# SCATTERING ASHES

# SCATTERING ASHES

## A MEMOIR *of* LETTING GO

*By*

JOAN Z. ROUGH

SHE WRITES PRESS

In order to maintain privacy for some mentioned in this memoir, I have changed their names or used initials to indicate their identity.

Published 2016
Printed in the United States of America
ISBN: 978-1-63152-095-2
Library of Congress Control Number: 2016934470

*Book design by Stacey Aaronson*

For information, address:
She Writes Press
1563 Solano Ave #546
Berkeley, CA 94707

She Writes Press is a division of SparkPoint Studio, LLC.

*To my mother, Josephine Zabski, and all mothers and daughters who are seeking to love and forgive each other.*

## CONTENTS

# PREFACE

WHAT DO YOU THINK ABOUT WHEN YOU BEGIN TO notice that your parents' hair is turning more white than gray, and that their heads nod like one of those wobbly dolls when you talk to them? How do you feel when they begin to visit the doctor's office weekly and are diagnosed with an ailment you've never heard of or may be terminal? What do you do when you notice all the dings and dents on the rear bumper of their car? And how do you handle their growing forgetfulness?

These are the hard questions all of us face as our parents age. Not only are they aging, we are, too. As we make decisions about eldercare for our parents, we also begin, reluctantly, to think about how we ourselves would like to be cared for as we enter the territory of old age. The answers and the options are all tough, but most of us don't get out of dealing with them, unless our parents—or we—die instantly in a plane crash while we're still fit to travel.

We can try denial. It's the easiest thing to do, for the moment. We can simply wait until the terminal diagnosis comes in—or until Mom or Dad plows their car into a tree or, worse, people standing on a sidewalk. Many of us want to take control by sending the ones who birthed us off to an assisted living facility or nursing home, but these options can leave us feeling sorrowful and guilty.

One October day in 2014, as I got in my car to go home after a Pilates session, I noticed a man lying on the ground in the parking lot. He had just fallen as he tried to fold his wife's heavy wheelchair and put it into the trunk of his car. The back of his head was scraped and bleeding. I helped the nurse who accompanied them out of the building to get him back on his feet. He complained that he had a "doozy of a headache." In the meantime, his wife struggled to hang onto her walker while she waited for someone to help her get into their car. While the nurse went back into the building to call the rescue squad, I stayed with the couple.

Both husband and wife were morbidly obese and appeared to be in their eighties. They both had extreme difficulty moving around, especially the wife. I was afraid the husband would fall again as he picked up his cane and started to sit in the driver's seat. "You've injured your head," I said. "I don't think it's a good idea for you to be driving." He replied, "I can handle it. I always do." When I suggested that a family member might be able to drive them to their appointments from now on, he replied, "They're no good. One won't work."

I went further, suggesting that they try the services of JAUNT, a community provider of transportation that many elderly people use, but he said, "I can't afford it. I don't have any money." He also said that they couldn't get free services because their income was a bit over $25,000 a year. He'd been told they had too much money to get help.

When the rescue squad arrived a few minutes later, the man denied having a headache and said, "I just want to go home." When asked, he admitted he had diabetes and a few other ailments but said he was sure he didn't have a concussion and refused to be taken to the hospital, adding, "Who will take my wife home? She can't drive."

In the meantime, the nurse called the couple's daughter, who arrived as the EMTs were examining her father. She stood by until the rescue squad left, then offered to drive them home. Her dad whined, "I'm okay. I can do it myself." As I left the parking lot, I watched the daughter kiss him on the cheek, then get into her car.

I was flooded with sadness and memories of having been my mother's caretaker during the final seven years of her life. It was difficult to watch those parents deal with the help their daughter offered. I also realized nothing has changed: The elderly are still as stubborn as ever about giving up their independence (I'm sure I'll do the same), and the broken systems that are in place to help some can't help others.

When babies are born, they don't come with a manual telling their new mothers how to take care of them. When we age, begin to fail, and need to be taken care of, there is no manual to tell our kids what to do with us. When my mother started falling on a regular basis and was diagnosed with a number of ailments, I began weighing the options. I could ignore the situation, I could try to convince her to go into an assisted living facility, or I could invite her to come and live with me.

Against advice from friends, I decided to go all the way and invite Mom to move in with me and my husband, Bill. I wanted to help. But as she grew more frail, our already difficult relationship turned into a mother-daughter war. I rued the day I'd brought her into my home. There was nothing I could do to console her as she got closer to death. There were moments when I wanted to throw her out. There were many days when I was afraid that I was losing my mind. My anxiety disorder held me in its grip so tightly that sometimes even my husband couldn't stand to be around me. And at times, much to my horror, I prayed that she would just die.

I'll never know how it would have turned out had I put her in an assisted living home or completely ignored the situation. The problem was that I loved her and wanted to make her final days as comfortable as possible. Little did I know that it would be one of the most difficult things I'd ever do.

Now, years later, I've come to understand that life has a way of taking us out of the ditch we've been living in to places of higher learning. During those hateful years, I learned about love, life, death, hate, and how to heal my own soul. I learned that forgiveness is not about forgetting. It is about coming to terms with the human spirit and what drives us to be the people we are. The story you are about to read is about how my mother and I worked our way through her last years, doing the best we could. It's a story about my growth and how I found love and forgiveness amid anger and hate.

# MOURNING DOVE

*May 21, 2007*

IT'S A BEAUTIFUL MAY MORNING IN VIRGINIA. THE grass is heavy with dew, and the air is filled with an early-morning concert by a choir of returning birds. They'll soon build nests in neighboring shrubs and trees, where they'll raise their young, then head south again in the fall, completing another yearly cycle.

As I turn the corner into my driveway, a mourning dove feeding on the ground takes flight. I feel a light bump as it collides with the hood of my car. I watch it rise straight up into the air, its wings outspread, surrounded in a veil of white light. When it vanishes into thin air, I know something has changed. It's a clear message that my mother is dead.

As I walk toward the house, I hear the phone ringing. My dear friend and housekeeper, Bobbie, greets me at the door and hands it to me. On the other end, the doctor tells me that Mom has just died. My two dogs, Molly and Sam, jump and yip at my feet, happy to see me. I've only been gone overnight, but they act as though it's been a month.

Once I'm alone, I call my husband, Bill, who's traveling in England. He'll be on the next flight out of Heathrow. Up in New England, my brothers, Zed and Reid, with whom I talked last night, are expecting my call. I phone my son, Mark, at nearby Cale Elementary School, where he teaches. When I reach my daughter, Lisa, in North Carolina, she is tearful. She's planning to be here tomorrow with the family.

The doctor and nurses have left Mom in her room so that I'll have as long as I need to sit with her and say my final goodbyes, but I'm in no hurry to rush back to the hospital where her lifeless body lies. Instead, I sit at home, looking out over the river, with a cup of tea and a slice of homemade bread still warm from the toaster. Both dogs are at my feet, begging for crumbs. I missed having them cuddled up next to me last night. The unconditional love of these two rescued mutts has helped me through many hard times. For the first time in seven years, I am free, no longer my mother's caretaker. It's been a long haul, and toward the end I prayed for the day when both Mom and I would be released from our pain.

Then yesterday, with all its discomfort, rushes toward me again. I was with her all afternoon and all of last night, as she began her journey to wherever people go when they die. Unbeknownst to me, she was admitted to the ER early yesterday morning. She'd complained to the nurse at the assisted living facility that her leg was badly swollen and she was in terrible pain. I discovered her missing after lunch when I stopped in to bring her fresh flowers and her favorite coffee ice cream.

If the nurse on duty had done her job properly, she'd have checked my mother's chart and called hospice directly. They would have arranged for an ambulance to deliver Mom to the hospital and into a private room, where her palliative pain management would have continued nonstop. Instead, the nurse called an ambulance herself and Mom was taken directly to the ER, where she did not receive her regular dose of pain meds. That same nurse also neglected to read that I was to be contacted immediately should Mom be sent to the hospital.

When I was told that Mom had been admitted around seven in the morning, I became a raging dragon. "What is wrong with you people? Why didn't you call me? It's right there in print on her chart." The nurse, still on duty, had nothing to say.

I found Mom moaning in the ER, in intense pain. A week earlier, as she'd pushed her walker out to the pond, where she could smoke without being caught, she had fallen, bruising her good leg. She'd been checked out by a doctor who said she'd be fine, but since then her leg had swollen to three times its normal size and looked like it was about to burst. Why hadn't the nurse in charge of Mom's care at the facility noticed?

Because the doctors weren't giving her the amount of morphine she needed to keep her comfortable, I explained that she was a hospice patient with untreatable lung cancer. No one seemed to hear me. One doctor told me that hospice wasn't welcome in the ER and refused to call them. Even after another doctor called the assisted living home to find out Mom's needs, the hospital still refused to give her the correct dose of morphine. When I asked why, I was told, "It will kill her." Furious, I yelled out in the middle of the emergency room, "She's a hospice patient! She *is* dying. Can't you see she needs more pain meds to keep her comfortable?" It made no difference. One of the nurses told me, "You need to leave. You're upsetting your mother," but when I asked Mom if she wanted me to go, she said no.

I called hospice myself and continued to harangue the doctors and nurses to help my mother be more comfortable. She was finally moved into a private room at around 5:30 p.m. Mom had been in the ER in excruciating pain, without proper care, for almost twelve hours.

After making sure that she was being given the correct dose of morphine, I rushed home to make a few calls. When I returned, Mom was propped up in bed, breathing in and out of an oxygen mask. An IV slowly delivered pain relief. There were other lines to monitor her heart and other bodily functions. An uneaten tray of food—chicken soup, a roll, and red Jell-O—sat nearby. On TV, the evening news was loudly reporting on the latest investigations into insider-trading deals. I turned it off, offered Mom a taste of Jell-O, but she was barely conscious.

Sensing that she was getting ready to make an exit within hours, I told her, "Mom, if you'd like to leave this world, you can go without worrying about Zed, Reid, or me. There is no reason for you to hang around if you wish to leave." With eyes closed, she nodded her head in understanding. I sat, holding her hand as she moved in and out of consciousness.

Suddenly, she sat up and said clearly, "You could say something, you know. Don't be afraid to talk."

I answered, "I'm not afraid to talk. I just want you to rest."

She replied, "Not you. Them," pointing at the empty wall she faced. Quickly settling back down, she closed her eyes, wandering off into an in-between world of sleep and wakefulness. I wondered if there really were family and friends waiting for her on the other side, as those who have had near-death experiences report.

Throughout the night, I dozed off and on in a huge recliner next to her bed. Her breathing was shallow and irregular. She occasionally called out in distress. I told her that I was there with her. A nurse came in several times to adjust the morphine drip. As the sun rose, her breathing became a bit more regular. The doctor suggested I go home, telling me there was plenty of time and that I really should have some breakfast. She promised to call immediately if anything changed.

I'M NOW SITTING BESIDE HER again. This time, her eyes are closed and she is no longer breathing. Her skin is an ashy gray. When I touch her arm, it is stone cold. The only sounds and movement in the room are from the still-inflating and deflating wrap that was placed around her swollen leg yesterday to keep blood clots from forming. It's as if she is still breathing somewhere beyond my understanding.

I feel only a touch of sadness. There are no tears. I try to talk to her about how difficult this last passage has been, but the pain is too fresh and I can't find words to describe what I feel. When the hospitalist comes in with her condolences, I find it easy to smile and thank her for looking after Mom. I can't allow my bitterness to show.

The following days unfold quickly. I have no time to lick my wounds or to sit with thoughts about the unending days I've given to my mother and her dying. As I make final arrangements to have her body cremated, as she wished, I try to breathe deeply, exhaling the angst and fear I've been holding in for so long.

Bill, along with our kids, removes Mom's belongings from her rooms at the assisted living facility. I contact faraway friends and relatives to let them know that she has passed on. When they ask me when and where Mom's burial will be, I promise that I'll let them know as soon as I know myself. My brothers won't be coming down from New England. They're waiting for me to tell them what's next. I'm still doing for Mom, even though she isn't here. Filled with resentment for being left with the responsibility for the remaining arrangements, I stash the brown plastic box holding Mom's ashes away on a shelf in the back of a storage closet, next to the Christmas decorations and old clothes that no longer fit. I slam the door closed.

But I can't get away from her. The last seven years replay over and over again in my head, like an old vinyl record that's stuck. Maybe I've missed something. If I move the needle back and start again, perhaps I will find out what it is.

# THE BEGINNING *of the* END

*August 2000*

WHEN MY FRIEND AND REAL ESTATE BROKER, PAT, calls to ask if he can show us a house that's been on the market for a year, I'm not terribly excited. "But the price has been lowered dramatically, and I know you'll love the location." He tells me the house is in a subdivision of eight homes and fronts the South Fork Rivanna Reservoir. I imagine the price will be way over what we're willing to spend, but one can look, hope, and dream.

Bill and I have been house hunting for about a month. Since our kids are grown and gone, we want to downsize and prepare for our elder years by finding a move-in-ready, one-story home. I also want to get far away from our new neighbors, whose barking dogs make getting a good night's sleep almost impossible. We've lived in central Virginia for twenty-five years and don't want to leave the area, but after looking at well over a dozen houses, we've about given up. There is nothing out there in our price range that we like.

Both Bill and I spent our early years living near or on the sea, and the water still calls to us and comforts us. If you believe in Darwin's theory of evolution, as I do, it's where we all began. If I am near enough to the ocean at night, I fall asleep easily to the whisper or roar of the waves. The opportunity to spend a night aboard a rocking boat is like being wrapped in the arms of the universe.

The house Pat wants to show us is a fixer-upper, but how can I say no to at least seeing a waterfront property? Our excitement grows when Pat tells us that the seller's agent told him, "Just bring us an offer—any offer." It's been shown only two or three times during the year it's been listed, and I wonder what's wrong with it. But my knowledge of the original asking price and of some of the work it needs leads me to believe it was too much for most buyers to take on and was not priced to sell.

At first look, the house is everything we don't want. It has five bathrooms, and several of the larger bedrooms have been split to create a total of seven bedrooms on the main and second floors. The basement level is completely unfinished except for a tiny studio apartment. The wear and tear on the place makes it quite obvious that the owners have been renting out rooms to UVA students.

The location is amazingly beautiful, on two and a half acres. There is a long, sweeping lawn down to the river, where a small dock would make it easy to launch our kayaks. In an orchard near the southern boundary grow several apple trees, along with a pear tree and a cherry tree. I notice the abundance of birds and the tiny pond off to one side of the house, inhabited by goldfish. Between the road and the front of the house is a grove of cedar trees that would be a beautiful place to set up an outdoor banquet table for summer feasts. But the size of the place, the work, and the money it would take to clean it up are far beyond what we're interested in.

Still, over the next few days, we can't get the river view, visible from every room in the house, out of our heads. Our wish to downsize is crumbling, and we start talking "location, location, location." Some days Bill says, "Let's go for it," while I say, "But it's so much work and way too big." The next day we reverse the dialogue, and then I find myself begging Bill to make an offer.

I'm blinded by desire. Deep down inside, I want that house. But it isn't a practical thing to do . . . unless we invite my mother to move in with us. Her health is failing, and I've been worried about her for a while now. She lives in her own home across town. She's had a few mini-strokes that have left her at risk of seriously injuring herself if she falls. It can often take me close to an hour to get to her house, especially if traffic is heavy. Buying this house would not only allow me to be at my mother's side within seconds but also scratch my itch to own this property.

When we visit the house a second time, I make note of the chair elevator on the stairs to the lowest level of the home. I suggest the possibility of rebuilding the apartment downstairs for Mom. To me, it seems like a practical solution to several issues, but Bill isn't happy with my idea. He reminds me, "You and your mother don't always get along. You'd have to be okay with having her around twenty-four hours a day. Also, redoing the lowest level of the house would increase our costs dramatically, and it would take much longer to finish rehabbing the place."

I admit that I'm a bit uneasy about living in the same house with Mom but also feel bad about her living alone. She often complains about being lonely, but I don't think moving her to an assisted living facility right now would make either one of us happy. My chronic guilt over my edgy relationship with her would bring me down for sure. When I suggest, "Rebuilding the apartment could bring in extra income in the future when Mom is gone and could also be a major selling point if we ever decide to move elsewhere," Bill caves, saying, "I'm willing to do whatever you want to do."

After several days of weighing the pros and cons and dealing with fear and angst about what the future might hold, I finally ask her if she would be interested in moving into a new place with us. She's coy at first, saying, "I'll consider my options." But when we take her to see what I hope will be our new home, she thinks it's a wonderful idea.

We make an insultingly low offer on the house, haggle just a tiny bit, and then the deal is done. We close on October 1 and immediately begin ripping the place apart. We put our current house on the market and sell it within two weeks. The new owner is willing to rent it back to us until the first of the year, when we'll move into our new home. Mom will put her house on the market next summer. Her new apartment will be the last thing we work on.

After all the papers are signed and the renovation begins, I wake up asking myself, *What the hell have I done? My mother, who is an alcoholic and extremely manipulative, is going to live with me!*

## LIVING *in a* CONSTRUCTION ZONE

*July 2001*

As SAWDUST PILES UP AND OLD WALLS ARE TORN down in our new house, the scene is all too familiar to me. I'm reminded of the feelings of impermanence that haunted my childhood as my family traveled like gypsies from one home to another.

It began when my father, young and gutsy, returned home to Long Island from World War II, ready to start his own business as an architect and homebuilder in a newly flourishing economy. He was the son of Polish immigrants and came of age in New York City during the Great Depression. He knew about poverty and planned to make a bundle of money so that his family would never have to live without food on the table or a roof over their heads.

It turned into a family affair, and by age six I was carrying and stacking lumber with the best of them, handily sweeping up dropped nails and sawdust at the end of each workday. The racket of table saws and boards being hammered into place were sounds I fell asleep to.

We moved continuously into partially finished homes that Dad built on spec. My folks would labor and sweat at completing each house, finally replacing the FOR SALE sign by the front door with one that read SOLD. As the last coat of paint was drying and the last door was being hung, we would pack and move into the next house that needed to be finished.

If there wasn't a house ready for us to camp out in, we'd move into a rental property for a while. By the time I was thirteen, I had lived in at least ten different homes and sometimes attended two or three different schools within one year. I was expected to greet each move with a smile, but I felt pushed and pulled along like the rest of the furniture. I mourned the loss of those kids who had become my best friends. They carried the secrets I'd told them, relieving the weight I carried on my shoulders. With each move, I repacked my secrets and moved on to the next place, hoping to find another friend I could share them with.

To complicate matters even further, my father suffered from post-traumatic stress disorder. The lessons he taught about life were dysfunctional and ill-conceived. He didn't have the slightest idea of how children operate and what they need in order to grow, and his role as a husband took on the style of an old-world "do as I say, not as I do," kingpin. To him, women and children needed constant direction from the men in their lives. All of us, including Mom, were horribly afraid of him. He spewed anger, often beating my brothers and me. Without exception, Mom would disappear when he brought out the belt or the leather horse crop he used on us. She never came to our rescue. One memory stands out in particular . . .

Hot, searing pain leaves me breathless and unable to connect my anguish with my father's hand. I move to the other side of the table, out of range, but he follows me, striking my back and legs again and again. I'm in shock, begging him to stop. When he's finished, I lie cowering on the floor, drenched in a pool of stinging tears.

Over time, the stripes of punishment turn from screaming red to deep purple, then fade to blue, then a sickly yellow-green. It hasn't ever happened this way before. He's hit me for my wrongs in the past but has never used the hard, braided leather crop that hangs in the back of his closet. Until now, it's only brought memories of a favorite story he often tells about the horse he kept during the war while he was in Germany.

Punishment isn't anything new to me. I've had my mouth washed out with soap numerous times, and if my room is a bit messy, he'll sometimes come in and sweep everything on my desk and bureau onto the floor and tell me to clean it up. I've been forced to stand at attention and listen to his ranting about how stupid I am. He has hit me before, but always with his hand and never with the violent intensity I experienced today.

I was thirteen years old then. I have no memory of what I did to be punished so harshly. The sudden shock of being beaten in that way obscured the many beatings that followed. I know they happened, but the details are hidden under a dark shroud of secret memories.

MY FATHER KEPT A MENTAL checklist of all of his requirements for his children. He insisted that I see my face reflected back at me in the toes of my freshly polished shoes. I was supposed to be able to bounce a quarter on my bed, illustrating that the sheets and blankets were pulled taut, with nothing hanging loose. He inspected my brothers and me for dirty fingernails, dirt behind our ears, and teeth that hadn't been brushed. He sometimes led us in push-ups, jumping jacks, running in place, and a host of other calisthenics he learned during his military training. We had to do it in sync, or we'd have to start all over again. We were to remain serious and follow orders at all times, no matter how we felt about what we were being directed to do.

He was around mostly on weekends and in the late evenings after he returned from work. He insisted that we take part in family work activities, like finishing up the house we were living in at the moment or clearing a wooded lot so that he could build another. If we got grades below a C, he punished us with no playtime and extra hours at our desks.

He treated Mom badly as well. They were constantly fighting over things I didn't understand. Though I never witnessed him beating her, I remember one chilly autumn evening when they were outside screaming at each other. I heard what sounded like someone hitting something hard. I ran out to find him throwing falls from our apple tree at Mom. He threw them so hard that they smashed to bits when they hit the tree behind her. Terrified, I ran and hid in my room until the raging stopped and silence intervened for the night. When I heard Mom drive off in the car, I was terrified that she'd never return. I lay awake most of the night, until I heard her car again, then fell asleep, relieved that I wouldn't be left alone with my father. I never knew whether he hit her or not. There were no visible signs that he had, but they didn't speak to each other for days on end. As usual, I was the one who delivered messages between them.

I loved and hated my father and feared being in his presence. As I got older, leaving his house was the first thing on my agenda. But after Bill and I got married, I began to see him and his violence for what they were: reactions to the unspeakable trauma he experienced during the war. He'd witnessed a buddy's head being blown off as they stood overlooking a field they thought was empty of enemy troops. Another time, he was the only survivor when he led an attack on a nest of German soldiers hunkered down somewhere in Italy. All of his men were killed. Back then, there was no such thing as PTSD. Soldiers who suffered from "shell shock" were left to themselves, experiencing unimaginable pain and leaving a trail of severe family abuse throughout the rest of their lives. No one in the government seemed to care.

When Mark and Lisa were tots, my father became their beloved Grampy Tom. While my brothers were obsessed with the damage he had done to them, my hatred for him slowly turned to compassion as I witnessed the consequences of the war in Vietnam. Soldiers, mostly my age, who returned alive, often suffered the same kind of damage my father had. It was impossible not to understand that war does horrible things to the minds and bodies of men and women when they fight with and kill other human beings.

By the time Dad was diagnosed with bladder cancer at age seventy, we had become friends. On a few occasions, he allowed his vulnerability to show in my presence. I knew he had done the best he could as a parent. His heart loved me. It was his screwed-up brain that caused his uncontrollable rage and violence. As he aged, I believe he began to understand for himself who he was. When he died, I felt nothing but love for him. Though I sometimes still feel angry at him, it is difficult to maintain. I have often felt akin to him, to his wild mood swings and explosive temper. Little did I know that I would one day be diagnosed with the same disease he suffered from.

I'M NOW IN MY FIFTIES and no longer a child. I'm supposed to be in control. But nothing is simple. Life's complexity grows, and the buzz around me is far too loud as I begin to come to grips with the fact that my mother has accepted our invitation to move in with us.

The apartment downstairs is beginning to take shape. The kitchen cabinets are up, and the appliances have been installed, along with a stacked washer and dryer. Granite countertops are being put in. The bedroom will have enough space for Mom's huge desk, and the bathroom will have an easy-to-get-into shower. We purchase a small gas stove for the living room.

Mom's move-in date of October 1 is getting closer. I'm hoping that by then I'll have some time to get myself into a daily creative routine, painting and making art in the large studio on the top floor of the house. But Mom's health is declining further. She's recently been diagnosed with temporal arteritis, a painful swelling of the vessels that supply blood to the head and neck region. She's had a few more mini-strokes, during which she blacked out and fell. She already has osteoporosis and emphysema and continues to smoke regularly.

She isn't yet using an oxygen tank, but I know there is one in her future. Her doctor has prescribed prednisone and the opiate painkiller Vicodin for the arteritis. For Mom, an alcoholic, just one glass of wine can open the door to the large load of anger that she carries around with her. Narcotics have the same effect. When she swallows that pill, she enters a continuous state of drunken rage.

I drive and accompany Mom to see her neurologist. I mention this particular problem, but the doctor isn't sure that there is any other drug that will relieve her pain without making her difficult to live with. While the doctor and I discuss the issue, Mom listens in, a picture of sweet innocence. I'm certain the doctor is looking at both of us, wondering which one of us is really the problem. I find it almost impossible to get anyone who doesn't know her as well as I do to understand how monstrous she can be when she's under the influence of drugs or alcohol.

I swing from truly wanting to make Mom's final years comfortable to remembering how easily we can annoy each other. As I've watched her decline, I've seen myself approaching old age and realized how afraid I am of aging and death. When she moves in, I will be reminded of it every day. Though I feel deep compassion for her, I need to remind myself that my chronic need to take on other people's problems keeps me from moving my own life forward. But her house is for sale and there is a lot of interest in it at the moment. She's counting on me.

When I share these thoughts with a close friend, she tells me, "Put her in an assisted living facility, where all of her needs will be addressed. You'll be worry free." While it's a tempting idea, I can't do that. I remember how I felt just a few years ago when Mom made her decision to move here to Virginia. While she waited for her house in New Hampshire to sell, she spent time with us getting to know this area, looking at senior communities where she might be happy. I visited assisted living facilities with her and walked with her through their nursing home wings. We saw grizzled old men and women slumped over in wheelchairs, not knowing where they were. It was deeply depressing for both of us. At that time, Mom didn't need such living arrangements. She was active, loved to garden, and spent her days in the woods, hunting for mushrooms. In New Hampshire, she was known for her ability to find morels when no one else could. And she impressed everyone with her fabulous cooking.

Being cut from the same piece of scratchy linen, we both agreed that she should buy a house. We strongly believed that, if at all possible, one should remain in the big, wide world surrounded by people of all ages, shapes, and sizes, instead of holing up in an old-fashioned old folks' home, where all one does is take drugs and wait for the final curtain to fall.

But living with me in the same house is a different matter. If this arrangement is to work, we both need to be careful about boundary issues. We're both extremely private people. We don't want to be stepping on each other's toes. I've already set up one house rule: there will be no smoking inside. We've also set up eating and cooking arrangements. Mom will join us for dinners that Bill or I will prepare three times a week. She will cook dinner and host us in her apartment twice a week. She'll be responsible for the rest of her meals, including breakfast, lunch, and all meals on weekends. She volunteers to pay for her share of the utility bills, but there are bigger, more deeply rooted issues, like her addiction and her tendency to manipulate those around her, especially me. All she has to do is pout a little, act the martyr, and I give in to her commands.

Not only are we in the process of reconstructing a new home for ourselves, we are also in the process of trying to rebuild our relationship.

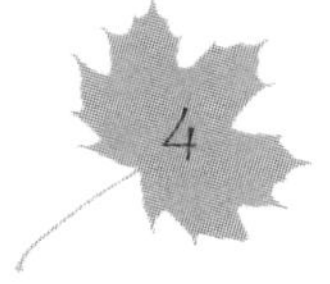

# SUMMER HEAT

*August 2001*

I'M HOME, EXHAUSTED, AFTER SPENDING THE MORNING with Mom. I drove her to see her neurologist this morning and then went back to her house to help her do some packing. I'm trying to be aware of what she needs. She isn't feeling well, and considering that she moved here from New Hampshire only a few years ago, I'm sure she isn't thrilled about all that has to be done so that she can move in with us.

She was low on patience today. If I asked her a question or made a suggestion, she snapped at me. The painkillers she's taking aren't helping. Rather than making matters worse, I decided to quit. I have lots of my own things to do at home. Maybe tomorrow will be better for her. I wound too easily to hang around now.

I know I need help with this situation. Asking for it is extremely difficult for me, but, knowing better, I decide to call a therapist I've worked with in the past. "Oh, I'm fine," I say, not being completely honest. "I just wondered if you might have some time to see my mother and me together. She's moving in with us in October, and there are a few issues we should probably work out before she comes." He's busy but recommends another therapist who has the time and is willing to see us.

I call Mom and cautiously broach the subject with her: "Hey, Mom, I thought it would be a great idea if we went to see a therapist together before you move in here. I want both of us to be comfortable living in the same house together. Sometimes we're impatient with each other, and I want to keep the peace."

To my surprise, she says breezily, "Sure. Why not? It'll be an interesting experience."

Our first appointment is on a typical hot, hazy, and humid summer day. I'm nervous, as I always am when I see a new therapist, and ask myself, *Why did I make this appointment?*

In the office, the shades are drawn against the heat of the day. Dr. Sears asks what she can do to help us. I begin with a brief summary of what is happening and gently voice my concerns. She asks my mother about hers, but Mom denies she has any and proceeds to tell the good doctor the story of her life. She talks about her childhood, about being poor, about her broken family and her own extremely abusive mother. Thankfully, she doesn't say, "I had only one dress, which was made from a grain sack." I've heard that one more than a million times. But Mom is unstoppable and is having a wonderful time. She loves telling her stories to anyone who'll listen and sympathize with her. I suppose the doctor needs to hear it all before she can begin to offer any help.

The hour is gone before I know it, and we make another

appointment. Beyond opening the discussion, I haven't made any other contributions to what has been said.

We meet the following week and again the week after that, and still it's all I can do to get a word in edgewise in any of the discussions. It's all about Mom and her childhood. It's about how her mother made her work as a maid and help put food on the table. It's about how her mother was declared unfit to raise her children, and the foster homes Mom and her siblings lived in. I'm angry and tired of hearing it. Neither Mom nor Dr. Sears seem to notice I'm in the room. I want to tell them about my life, but whenever I make a stab at talking about my needs, Mom says, "Don't worry. It's going to be okay."

She doesn't have the faintest idea of who I am. I want to tell her, "I feel strangled when you shush me and try to keep me from speaking my truth." I want to tell her that my heart breaks when I see her drinking. I want her to know that I care about her. At an early age, I was taught that if something is problematic, you don't cry, you don't complain, and you never ask for help. Still, she needs to know how difficult my own life has been. It wasn't that long ago when my brothers and I were visiting with her, discussing how Dad beat us, and Mom said, "Don't be silly. That just isn't true." She'd blocked those incidents completely out of her mind and remembered only her own misfortunes. There have been so many times when I have wanted to ask her, "What kind of mother are you, allowing your husband to beat your children until they were black and blue?" But I haven't.

I've made a terrible mistake in asking for help. We both have difficult stories to tell, but the therapist has been completely taken in by "lovely" Mom. Doubting my own inner wisdom, I sometimes wonder if I'm selfish and am simply overreacting. Then I tell myself, *No, this just isn't working. Let's just quit while we're ahead.* I decide our next visit will be our last.

At the next meeting, I try to take a bit of control of the conversation. As I begin to speak, I can't help but burst into tears. Before I can say much of anything, Mom shushes me and reaches over to give me a hug, saying, "Don't cry. You know I love you." Dr. Sears smiles at a job well done.

# FAMILY DYNAMICS

*September 2001*

As I PREPARE MYSELF FOR MOM'S MOVE INTO HER apartment downstairs in just two weeks, memories from the past fill my head. I'm caught up in a multitude of questions about how sharing my space with her will work. Despite my fear of her being here with me, I'm also excited. Perhaps it will be a good thing and we will begin to reconnect in a more loving way. People observing us from afar often comment on how close Mom and I seem. It always surprises me, because we are close only in that I am a vessel into which I allow her to pour her own challenges. I hold them for her, always there, a container she fills with her anger and disappointments. They are more than a distraction. I have my own problems, but I focus on Mom, who "needs" me. That is my addiction. The truth is that even when someone tells us we look so alike, I want to reply, *Thanks, but I'm not anything like my mother and I don't want to be!*

The oldest and only girl in a family of three siblings, I became my parents' go-between at an early age. Their match was a difficult one. My father, the child of immigrants, held on to his parents' old-world values, marrying a woman who not only was beautiful but also seemed submissive. I believe Mom felt trapped in her life. Uneducated and feeling desperate, she may have believed that he was her knight in shining armor, the hero who would rescue her from poverty and despair. Little did either one of them know that the state of the world would intrude on their dream of a happy partnership, bringing more abuse to Mom's life when my father returned from the war, suffering from a broken spirit.

Because her own mother had been abusive and absent at times, Mom's mothering skills sometimes left something to be desired. I watched as she set an example of how a wife gives her all to her husband. I learned to be a "good girl" and how to keep the family peace. She taught me how to cook and sew. I was expected to take care of my brothers when she was busy. It gave me power. Paying little attention to my own difficulties, I felt like Wonder Woman, the family shrink, loaded with wisdom and knowing what's best for everyone.

My parents considered me the stable child in the family. I graduated from college with a bachelor of science in elementary education and then married a "good" man who could take care of me. I was what my parents wanted me to be, and I wanted their approval more than anything else. I was caught in a family dynamic that was abusive and controlling. I ended up joining the ranks, wanting to have control over my own life as well as the lives of all those around me. I couldn't allow myself to mess up. I was a perfectionist. They all depended on me. Or so I thought.

My brothers, on the other hand, never produced the results Mom and Dad expected. They never finished college. They let their hair grow and joined the ranks of the counterculture, wanting little to do with their parents' world. They grew and smoked pot and jumped from job to job. When my father tried employing Reid, the youngest, to run the motel he owned, they battled constantly. Reid wouldn't follow the letter of the law my father laid out for him and finally walked off the job. When Reid was certain he would be drafted and sent to Vietnam, he moved to Canada until the war was over. Although Dad didn't support that war, he was a veteran, so I imagine he was a bit disappointed in his son.

Early on, Zed took off for parts unknown. He drove a semi cross-country for a while, lived in a commune on the West Coast, and then moved on to Mexico. He didn't call home for months at a time. Mom was heartbroken, worried that he was dead or in jail. In my parents' eyes, Reid and Zed were irresponsible. They were "the boys" who couldn't hold it together and shunned the politics, wealth, and influence that the 1950s and '60s had produced. Their relationship with my parents turned into a mutual war of words.

Bill and I were married in 1965, one week after I graduated from college. We lived in St. Johnsbury, Vermont, well over an hour away from Killington, where my folks had been building and running ski lodges for years. The distance was enough to keep us from seeing each other on a regular basis, but Mom called often, sometimes three or four times a week. Her calls usually came between four and six in the evening. I could always tell that she was drinking by her slurred speech. These were not your usual happy family conversations. They typically came after a fight that she'd had with my father, or with one or both of my brothers. I tried to be neutral, but there were times when I had to agree with what she had called to complain about.

During those often-dreaded conversations, I listened as I prepared dinner for my own family, saying "uh-huh" when it felt appropriate. I tried not to get sucked into the drama, but I always ended up in a stew of my own, angry and aghast at my family members' behavior. I didn't realize that I was helping to feed a hungry wolf who lived on juicy tidbits of family gossip.

At the same time, there was turmoil and confusion in the United States as the feminist movement took hold. Mom lived her "crappy" life, watching with disapproval as younger women burned their bras, entered the workforce, and demanded equality in every phase of their lives. I eagerly cheered them on while at the same time I clung to the old ways as a frustrated stay-at-home mom, disappointed that I had never taken the opportunity for some independent living before I got married.

Eventually, the difficult role I had taken on began to tear me apart. I felt trapped in a world I had no control of, doubted that being a mother and wife was what I really wanted, and was often depressed. I had always thought of myself as ahead of the game, in control, with a solution for every problem. I sweet-talked, openly took sides, and gave advice. In the end, my part in the fraying of relationships within my family of origin was not appreciated, and a large rift developed between my brothers and me.

When Bill and I moved to Virginia, Reid accused us of abandoning the family. Because we could afford to build a new solar home on a large piece of land, they both snidely called our place the Ritz of the South. We rarely spoke to or saw each other. I called them on major holidays to wish them well, and

Mom happily filled the silence with reports of the nasty things that one or the other said about me.

When my father died of bladder cancer in 1981, Mom's calls became all about her loneliness. Zed and Reid lived near enough to Mom to see her frequently but failed to be a helpful presence in her life. She often invited Reid, who lived the closest, for dinner. More often than not, he arrived with a few friends, having never informed Mom to expect extra mouths to feed. If Reid or Zed was in trouble, she paid their bills, complaining to me every step of the way. They rarely honored her on Mother's Day or on her birthday, and I listened to the litany of their neglect at long-distance rates, until my empathic soul was filled to the brim with everyone else's problems.

Mom's slurring of words increased as she began to drink more. Then, on the anniversary of my father's death, soused out of her mind, she fell down the cellar stairs and broke her hip. Aware that she was lonely and lacking much family support, I suggested that she consider moving to Virginia.

Living twelve hours away from my family of origin had been a blessing, but when Mom took me up on my suggestion, I felt as if I had betrayed myself. I was busy with my own interests, exploring my place in the world of fine-art photography. I was taking care of myself, not worrying about anybody else. I had sought out therapists who were helping me with my anxiety and bouts of depression. I was learning new things about myself, and when Mom said she wanted to come to Virginia, I found myself asking, "What the hell were you thinking?"

Once again, I'm asking myself that same question.

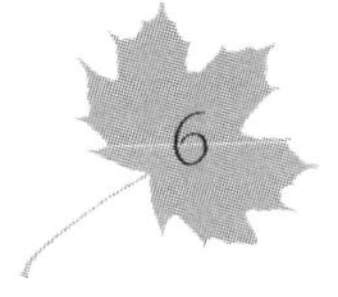

# 6

## JUST FINE

*May 2002*

MOM HAS BEEN LIVING IN HER APARTMENT SINCE last October. Because she's doing well on her own, Bill and I took two weeks to head south to sunny, warm Florida in January. We enjoyed the days being by ourselves. But a few days into our travels, Mom fell and broke her wrist. Thankfully, the house sitter I'd hired to take care of the dogs and keep an eye on her was able to handle the situation. I was grateful that we didn't have to rush home before we were rested. But, always trying to be the perfect daughter, I spent too much of my vacation time feeling guilty that I wasn't there for her.

I was reminded that a number of years ago, when Mom fell while ice-skating and broke her hip, I did not rush up to New Hampshire to be by her side. Instead, I spent several months feeling horribly disrespectful and uncaring, even as her older sister was taking good care of her. I don't know what to do with the guilt I carry for things I can't control. With Mom living downstairs, how do I keep from owning her problems and making myself crazy?

While I shrink into my new role as a guilt-riddled caretaker, Mom goes out on her own to work out at a nearby gym and visits with friends. She has volunteered at the local SPCA, stuffing envelopes and helping to organize its annual fundraising event. The rest of the time, she reads, watches golf on TV, and creates greeting cards for birthdays, Valentine's Day, and whatever other celebratory days come along. Every now and then she'll start knitting or get back to work on a quilting project she set aside months ago. She seems happy most of the time, but sometimes the sad look on her face gives away her loneliness. She is grieving her losses as she finds herself moving, uncontrollably, into old age. When she recently had surgery to repair a hernia and wasn't able to drive, Bill or I took her to her appointments. With her independence disrupted, she became the Wicked Witch of the North. For every ray of sunshine, she produced a black cloud. Bill and I kept our worries about the future to ourselves.

Now all of us, including Mom, are noticing that her memory is slipping. Yesterday she told me that she had an appointment today to have her hair done. This morning, she came upstairs terribly upset. "Um, that appointment I had for today was yesterday." Confused, she stumbled over her words, as she tried to hang onto a bit of dignity.

As her memory lapses occur more frequently, her shame is hard for her to hide, but she finds asking for help to be abhorrent. Her constant, wet cough is getting worse and is a sinister clue to what could lie ahead. Though she can still be very much her own person, she now and then acts like a child, seeking attention by asking for help with things that she knows how to do. If she doesn't like the way I'm helping, she attacks, saying, "Leave me alone. I'll take care of it. You obviously don't know what you're doing." Everything in her world must be just so, and if I don't commit to her way, I get in trouble.

I'm secretly terrified that someday I will find myself in the same predicament, but I try not to think about it. I know that this is all going to get much worse. I shouldn't complain, and I try to banish all signs of negativity from my head. But I'm only human. I'm afraid these small irritations will soon take on the size of a bull elephant chasing me through a jungle of worries.

Mom is still strong-willed and wants desperately to be independent. If you inquire whether she is a Republican or a Democrat, she will erupt in anger because you've asked her a stupid question. She used to laugh about her political preferences, but now she says, "Everyone should know by now that I'm an Independent. I refuse to support *any* political party." One day I found her watching Rush Limbaugh, whom I knew she hated with a passion. When I asked, "Why are you listening to someone who makes you so angry?" she replied, "I need to know what the other side is thinking."

When we're out in public, Mom is famous for making embarrassing comments that everyone around her can hear. I'm never sure if she wants others to hear her judgments or if she doesn't realize that she's speaking so loudly. One of her more awkward moments was when we were looking for seats at the movies one afternoon. We finally sat down next to a man who had overused his aftershave lotion. "Who stinks?" was the first thing out of Mom's mouth, as she stared directly at him. I quickly moved to another seat, several rows away from her.

On another occasion, having decided to have lunch outdoors so we could enjoy the gorgeous spring afternoon, we found a table at an outdoor café. Our waitress was a young woman dressed in black, with black nail polish, dyed black hair, and a rather strange-looking black tattoo on one of her legs. As she moved away from our table after she delivered our menus, Mom commented, "That tattoo is stupid, and her black fingernails are disgusting." When I countered, "It's her choice and none of our concern," Mom turned on me. "What? Can't you see that there is obviously something wrong with that girl? You should know better."

These are the times when I hate my mother. She makes me want to hide under the table or run like hell, screaming, "I don't know that woman! She doesn't belong to me!" However, I'm supposed to be the sane one here.

When I invited Mom to move in with us, my intention was to care for her as she aged and became frail. I believed that being her advocate during visits to the doctor would be a good thing. I believe in asking questions and being honest, but she quickly gets passive-aggressive when I report the fact that she smokes and is an alcoholic. She'd never volunteer that information on her own, though doctors need to know. I want to help her, but "helping" in Mom's mind is about agreeing with everything she says and wants to do.

Though I'm not aware that she's been drinking since she's been with us, you never know what might trigger her need for a glass of wine or a shot of scotch. With Mom, just a little goes a long way to bring out her feistiness and aggression. In her eyes,

I'm sure she sees me take on the characteristics of my father or someone else who abused her in the past. I know that alcoholism is a disease. It's not something she does on purpose to make me daft. But I can't find a place in my heart that feels love and compassion for her when she gets boozy and hostile. I've done time in Al-Anon and know all the words that are supposed to help. Even though I often repeat, "Let go and let God" and the Serenity Prayer, the words don't seem to help much when it comes to dealing with my mom.

At times, being her caretaker has been easy and I've been able to supply her with what she needs, but it's getting harder. It brings out the "perfect daughter" routine I know so well. I still want to please her but find myself feeling ashamed and wanting to cower when she criticizes me. However, I'm a grown woman now. I shouldn't cower before anyone. I'm supposed to be strong and in charge of myself. But her anger turns me into a six-year-old. As a caretaker, I'm not supposed to feel frustrated, angry, hateful, helpless, or afraid of the person I'm taking care of.

I constantly tell myself everything will be fine: *The earth is continuing to rotate. The stars still shine, even on cloudy nights. Mom is fine. I am fine*. But if you've ever attended Alcoholics Anonymous or Al-Anon meetings, you know that "fine" means "fucked up, insecure, neurotic, and emotional."

# MOM'S STORY

*Spring 2003*

DESPITE MY MOTHER'S MORE-THAN-ANNOYING behaviors, I don't want to give up on her. Just before she moved in with us, I invited her to make a DVD on which she could tell her stories. I thought that if I could get her to let her hair down and speak from her heart, we'd be better prepared to live together. Having no written records of her life, except for her birth and marriage certificates, I believed future generations might be interested in knowing more about her. I also imagined that the opportunity to be "onstage," without an obvious audience, might allow her to be more open. I knew many of her stories, but there was much that she kept hidden. My hope was that she would finally speak the fact that she'd been badly mistreated and be able to talk about her feelings. I thought she would then understand that her misfortune impacted our entire family. I hoped she would see her life in a new light.

Not wanting to influence what she said, I stayed in the background while a friend did the filming and asked her a list of questions we had put together. There were no tears, no "aha" moments—only the same old stories she'd told in the same old way, year after year. They were like loads of dirty laundry that she put through the wash over and over again. But in the end they always came out looking the same: stained and filthy. She showed us the dirt but never removed it. She couldn't let the pain out of her life and carried it with her always. No new details arose. The gaping holes in her timeline were still there. We had both experienced trauma and abuse as children and, later, at the hands of my father. I'd hoped we'd find some common ground to help each other build a new relationship.

Mom did have a tumultuous upbringing as one of four children. According to what she told me, her father, whom she loved dearly and who was a devout Catholic, had been preparing for the priesthood in Poland but was sent to the United States to wed her mother, in an arranged marriage. Her mother was quite young, perhaps only fifteen, when they married.

It was never a happy union. Years into the marriage, they split up when a serious disagreement arose between them one morning while the family sat around the breakfast table. Mom's mother, known for her short temper, picked up a hot iron skillet and threw it at her husband. The skillet barely missed my mother's head before landing on the floor without hurting anyone. When her father left the room, Mom followed him to his room, where he threw his belongings into a baby carriage. He wheeled it down the street to a neighbor's home as Mom ran after him in tears, begging him not to leave. My grandmother was left to raise her kids as a single mother.

Some time later, without knowing why, Mom and her siblings were sent to live with their grandmother. Later, they moved back home, only to be split up and sent to different foster homes. Their mother was reported to be unstable and unfit to raise her children. Mom told me, "I never knew where my mother was." Her disappearance became a deep, dark family secret that no one talked about. To this day, her whereabouts are still a mystery. In her teens, Mom returned home again to live with her mother. "She kept me from going to school, so I could help put food on the table working as a maid," she recalled. But her mother threw her out of the house on a number of occasions, telling her, "You're too much trouble to have around."

AT AGE SIXTEEN, MOM FOUND herself kicked out permanently. She took a job in a lace factory and moved in with her older sister, who was already married and had a family. A year or so later, Mom met my father, and, after a seven-month courtship, they were married on Valentine's Day in 1942. The day following their wedding, my father enlisted in the army and went off to train for the First Special Service Force. He fought in Europe to bring Hitler down. I was born nine months later.

When my dad was fighting in Europe, Mom and I had no home of our own. We lived for a short while with his parents, but, aware that Mom's mother was mentally unstable, they often bullied her with remarks like "The apple never falls far from the tree." When they accused her of cheating on my father and locked her out of their home, we moved in with close friends and then, later, back to Mom's older sister's home.

We always had a roof over our heads, but it was never our own. Many of the people with whom we stayed have since told me that I spent the first years of my life constantly crying, clinging to my mother. I'm sure the continuous stress Mom was under affected me even before I was born and is at the root of my own anxiety and panic disorder.

We began living together as a family when Mom and I joined my father in Germany, when I was four years old and he was doing postwar intelligence work. My memories of that time are few, but those I'm able to recall are of a sweet and loving home. Dad often took us up into the Alps, where he taught me how to ski. I spent lots of time sitting in his lap. I felt warm and snug with this new person in my life. We had rarely seen each other since my birth; he had simply been the man in the picture who wore a strange-looking uniform and was said to be my dad.

I remember having felt especially loved and wanted on one occasion, tucked between Mom and Dad in a horse-drawn sleigh, as saucer-size flakes of snow fell and melted on the sheepskin rugs that covered our laps. I learned to speak German fluently and became my mother's translator. I played with little girls my own age who spoke no English. We created chains of wildflowers to wear on our heads. I ate meals at their dinner tables and went to church with them. They were very kind and happy to have Americans in their midst.

One of the rare times I saw Mom exhibit deep sorrow about her past was the evening she came to me, describing what she thought had been a dream. "Maybe it was a dream, but something in my gut tells me it really happened," she said. She was confused and wanted to ask me what I thought. In a teary voice, she explained, "One morning, when I was very small, my mother gathered us kids together and took us outside to play near the railroad tracks that ran behind our house. In the distance, I could hear a train whistle. I was happy—I loved to wave at the trains as they went by—but as it approached, my mother pulled us onto the tracks and said, 'Let's play ring around the rosie.' My uncle, who was nearby, saw what was happening and rescued us before the train could do its damage and wipe out my family."

Before she told me about it, Mom called her siblings to ask them if it was true. They all said they didn't have any memory of such an event. The uncle who was the hero had died years earlier. She was left carrying this chilling story that she intuitively felt was real. After Mom died, my cousin told me it was. Her mother had told her the same story just before she died. It's definitely a clue about why my grandmother was considered an unfit mother, and it says much about the family's state of denial.

I was never aware as a young child that my mother was a lush. It wasn't until I was a young adult living far from home and returning for holidays that I noticed her drinking and the tirades that followed. She was trapped in midlife, wondering what she had done all those years. When the pain of holding in her frustrations, disappointments, and my father's neglect and abuse became unbearable, Mom self-medicated with a glass of wine, a shot of scotch, or a cold beer. It made her feel better and less fearful. The booze allowed her to speak her anger and hatred.

UNDER SWEET ALCOHOL'S INFLUENCE, SHE became a tornado, destroying everyone in her path. It was especially horrifying when we ate out at restaurants. As Mom slowly sipped a drink, usually a martini, the wind would pick up, encircling us, as well as those seated at tables nearby. She became loud and bullied my father or whoever else had made her angry that day. If any of us tried to quiet her, her voice got louder and we tried to melt into the ether. It wasn't until Dad spoke loudly and asked the waiter to bring the check that it was over. Then, back home, the shouting, accusations, and denial blew up into a perfect storm, sometimes with glasses and dishes flying across rooms. Threats of leaving forever filled the night, until Mom could no longer keep her head up and went to bed, fully clothed and sobbing. Most mornings, she woke exhausted and feeling bad but not remembering what had happened the night before. Unconsciously relieved of the pain that she couldn't keep from overflowing, she would become her usual pleasant self. In order to stay out of her way, I became an expert at smelling the tiniest bit of alcohol on her breath before it was too late and her fury rose to destructive levels.

While Mom was still living up north, she called me one evening in tears. She'd obviously been drinking and couldn't contain her grief. She told me that a gentleman she'd been dating and whom she cared for very much had just called to say he didn't want to see her again and that he was getting married. I imagined that her drinking habits might have become a problem for him; then again, I had no idea that she'd even been seeing anyone. After my father died, Mom announced she'd never marry again, saying, "I don't want to wash men's dirty socks anymore. I've had enough of that." I found her metaphor amusing; dirty socks meant nothing when it came to dealing with my father. Despite his abuse, she was lonely after he died but apparently changed her mind, keeping her hot dates a deep, dark secret. That night, between bouts of tears, she told me, "I was sure that he was going to propose to me. I loved him and would have said yes."

I spent almost an hour talking with her; I assumed the role of the mom while she played the part of a lovesick teenager. All I could say to her was, "I'm so sorry." She eventually stopped crying and abruptly hung up the phone, saying, " I need to go to bed now." She never spoke of the man or that evening again.

As I begin looking at my own past, I know there are memories I've locked up in my own subconscious, where they can't bring me nightmares. I wonder if they will remain safely tucked inside me or if I will be able to let them out one day. There have been traumas in my life I've heard about but have no memory of, like the maid who took care of me when we lived in Germany. I was told she panicked every time a plane flew overhead. She'd grab my arm and drag me through the house to the basement, trying to find shelter, sure that bombs would be dropped on us. Because I spent large amounts of time with her, I followed her example and was terrified as well. When my parents discovered what was happening, they fired her. It wasn't until twenty years later, when I revisited Germany on my honeymoon, that my mind was suddenly flooded with remembered images of the bombed-out buildings and piles of rubble that filled the landscape while I was living there.

I find it sad and ironic that I spend so much of my own time encouraging my mother to remember the hard times in her life while I run from my own demons, hiding from my own story.

# TRAVELING COMPANIONS

*Summer 2004*

MOM'S COUGH IS DEEP, WET, AND GRAVELLY. SHE has difficulty breathing at times. Canisters of oxygen are now being delivered to the house every two weeks. She also has a portable tank that she can carry with her when she goes out. But she isn't tempted to go anywhere. Ashamed of her poor health, she goes only to the grocery store or to get her hair done. She complains, "These are supposed to be my golden years. Where's the gold?"

She has emphysema but is still smoking. When she visits her doctors, she likes to tell them, "I quit." But, much to her dismay, I'm always there to set the record straight. She's like a five-year-old who insists upon crossing the street without stopping to look and listen before dashing out into traffic. She consumes large numbers of pills, uses an inhaler, and doesn't listen to her doctor when he tells her to quit. I've sometimes asked her, "Are you trying to kill yourself? Isn't there a quicker way?"

Now I've finally decided to let myself off the hook and stop nagging her. What's the point? It's her life. But one day, shortly after I made that decision, I caught her standing in the shade, just outside her door, smoking, while hooked up to her oxygen tank inside. I shouted, "What the hell are you doing, Mom? Do you want to blow up the house? Just don't take me with you, lady." I was once a two-pack-a-day person myself. Smoking is an addiction. But if I can quit, so can she. You'd think she'd want to, especially since her doctor told her that cigarettes will one day be the cause of her death.

At the moment, I see myself as a stupid middle-aged woman who has given up her own life to take care of the unfortunates around her so that she doesn't have to face her own demons. But I'm a fraud and no Mother Teresa. I want my life back. I want to be able to go out and not have to worry about being back in time to take care of someone. I want to live a spontaneous life, stopping to watch the sunset or taking as long as I want to chat with friends over lunch.

I watched my father go through a regrettable death in which he never came to terms with how he had spent his life or the bitter relationships he had with his sons. What keeps me from running away now is that I'd like to see my mother have a better ending. But when I'm feeling trapped, overwhelmed, and sorry for myself, I tend to forget that.

There are times when I absolutely hate the woman. Her incessant negativity takes me down with her, and I wonder how much longer it will be before she dies. Will she ever realize that

I've been a good daughter, even though I didn't meet all of her wants and wishes? I fear my own end of life and the long, painful aging process that could leave me like her, broken and remembering only times of despair. I wish I had someone to show me how to navigate my own aging and death so that I won't become an old, ungrateful hag. Sometimes I'd like to shake her and say, *Mom, please help me.*

In my more rational moments, I feel deep love and compassion for her and find it heartbreaking to watch her slip away. It makes me think of all the dogs and cats I've put to sleep. I know how the light goes out in their eyes. I know they won't sit in my lap, purring, or wag their tails for me when I return from a trip. I know the emptiness, the desperation of loss, and the need to fill the hole in my heart before I bleed to death.

In a desperate moment of trying to make her happy, I wonder if seeing her great-grandchildren—Zoe, now four, and Noah, age one—would help. But Lisa can't bring them here to visit anytime soon. So Bill and I decide to take Mom to visit them instead. It's a six-hour trip. We're not sure it's a great idea but figure it can't hurt—it will get her out of the house and perhaps lighten her spirit. When I propose the idea to her, she's excited.

I plan the trip carefully so she'll be comfortable, arranging for an oxygen tank to be in place when we arrive at the house we'll be renting. The hours in the car are long, the weather is hot, and Mom is fussy. She complains, "I just want to get there." I'm worried we've asked too much of her.

I remember a trip I took with her years ago. It was after Dad died and before Mom moved to Virginia. A weaver at the time, I planned on joining a group of other fiber artists on a once-in-a-lifetime trip to Peru and Bolivia to meet native weavers and explore places like Machu Picchu.

Mom was lonely, still mourning my dad, and trying to figure out what to do with her life. This was my first big adventure outside the United States on my own. The idea of being without a friend or family member was a bit daunting. I reasoned that the company of someone I already knew would be comforting, and I imagined it might open up the world for Mom, so I invited her to come along. Perhaps she would discover that her life wasn't over because her husband was gone. I looked forward to her company and to sharing new experiences and perspectives with her.

While I made friends and conversed with the others in the group, Mom hung out with two women about her age. Gloria and Jean were nice enough, but, along with Mom, they stayed in the background, whispering among themselves. Though she tried to hide it, I noticed Mom having a cocktail or two before our evening meals. Not wanting to cause one of her destructive tornados, I didn't say a word and tried to stay away from her at mealtime.

On the third day of our tour, Mom decided to stay at our hotel instead of visiting Isla Taquile, in Lake Titicaca, where we would have the opportunity to watch and talk with local weavers who created colorful, hand-woven rugs. She wasn't feeling well, and I agreed that it would be good for her to stay behind and rest. When I returned later in the day, excited to tell her about all that I had learned, she greeted me with rage. She didn't say it, but it was clear that she resented having been left behind. She ranted at me for almost thirty minutes about the "nasty" hotel and the fact that they didn't supply washcloths (only hand and bath towels) for their guests. She screamed, "You have some nerve, bringing me to this horrible third-world country. They eat guinea pigs here. That is disgusting!" I tried to calm her down, but she tore into me with all of the energy she could muster yelling, "You're a Goody Two-Shoes." When I got close enough to get a whiff of her breath, I knew what the problem was.

We were sharing a room. I was tired, needed to kick back, and had no place to get away from her. I tried reasoning with her: "We're on a wonderful adventure, and the people we're meeting are beautiful. We are guests here, and their culture is different from ours." She screamed back, "I don't care. Guests should be supplied with washcloths." She was spiraling out of control; I was afraid she'd start throwing things.

Her face bright red, she paced back and forth as her tirade continued. I sat on the bed, too scared to move. Such was her power when she drank and raged. I was afraid that people in the hall and in the rooms on either side of us would hear her and come to the door to see what was wrong. I had to do something to stop her from destroying what, up until then, had been a wonderful, life-changing trip for me.

Knowing that saying anything more would only make her anger worse, I pasted on a smile, rose from the bed, and quickly made my way to the door, saying, "I'll be back in a little while." Filled with shame and afraid that the others in the group would figure out that Mom was an alcoholic, I joined my other traveling companions sipping glasses of wine in the hotel bar. When they asked if Mom was feeling better, it was all I could do to keep myself from bursting into tears and telling my new friends what had just happened. Thankfully, Mom did not join us for dinner and was asleep when I tiptoed back into our room later in the evening.

The next morning, Mom behaved as if nothing had happened. I'd been in similar situations with her before, but never without Bill nearby. Calm and laid-back, he often helped me work my way through Mom's outbursts. Here I had no support. I wasn't sure if she really didn't remember the way she had behaved or if she was in complete denial about it. And I wasn't about to ask. I distanced myself from her as the rest of our time together slipped away. I was stressed, always waiting for her next explosion. My body ached and felt as though I'd been hauling around a ten-ton boulder. After that experience, I swore I'd never travel with her again. But now here I am, escorting her to the mountains of North Carolina.

The weather is gorgeous, and the place we've rented is one of several cabins surrounding a lovely pond, complete with trilling frogs and turtles basking in the sun. Despite the peaceful environment, I'm on edge looking after Mom's needs. She looks a bit unhinged and tires more easily than usual. I'm having second thoughts about having brought her here. I can tell she's uncomfortable. She misses her own bed and her daily routine.

One afternoon, we take Mom to visit with Lisa in her home. I'm already feeling stressed because I haven't had any alone time for three or four days. Bill is caught up in keeping the peace between Mom and me. When she spots a person walking by on the street, she asks, "Is that a man or a woman walking that little dog?"

Uninvited words stream out of my mouth. "How in the world can you drive a car when you can't see that the person is a man and he's walking a large German shepherd?" Mom immediately explodes into a torrent of nasty words.

Knowing that her eyesight has been getting bad, I recently tried to start a conversation with her about driving and giving up her license. But, curling her lip like a mad dog, she wanted none of it and I was too afraid to push it any further. I was concerned because she was constantly taking her car to the body shop to get numerous dents and dings fixed. Whenever I asked about them, she explained, "Other people are always backing into me when I'm at the grocery store." I'm worried about being responsible for any accident she might cause in which some other person is hurt.

In the midst of the shouting, Lisa ushers Zoe and Noah to their bedrooms for a nap. Bill tries to calm me down, but I feel betrayed by his words of blame. He's taking my mother's side and telling me to settle down. Feeling out of control, and enraged by being shushed, I grab the car keys, sitting on the coffee table, and drive off, leaving Bill and my mother behind.

I go back to our cabin, where I spend an hour walking around the pond, listening to the loud voice in my head beating me up for losing control and being just like Mom. At the same time, another voice, as loud as the first, curses both my mother and Bill for making me feel so inept.

After jotting a few angry notes in my journal, I conclude that I'm the one who caused the ruckus. Deep down, I know I was mean to my mother, but I reason that she's always mean to me. Still, I know I need to make amends. When I return to Lisa's, all conversation stops when I walk in. Everyone looks at me as though I've committed a heinous crime. I have no allies here, but, staying composed, I apologize for my blowup. “I’m so sorry,” I say. “There is no excuse for my behavior.”

We spend another day with Lisa and the grandkids, before heading home a day early. We’re all exhausted, and I’m still angry and filled with humiliation, but I’m ultra-polite to Mom. This time, she hasn’t forgotten what happened yesterday. She’s in control, and when we’re alone she throws poison darts my way, in the form of cutting remarks. I take them without wincing, knowing that there is nothing else I can do.

Once we’re home and unpacked, I rush to my studio, where I splash red, yellow, and black paint onto large pieces of canvas. As I release my shame and anger, trips I took with Mom when I was living at home and before I was married come to mind. We’d happily get in the car and drive across New England, antiquing together. She purchased treasures for her shop, Carousel Antiques, while I collected old kitchenware, teapots, and an Ironstone pitcher and bowl for the home that Bill and I would soon inhabit together. I loved those trips with Mom and was always amazed by her sense of history and her ability to resurrect worn-out pieces of what some would have called junk.

Now, as Mom enters the period others have named the end of life, I am trying to stay by her side. The journey is not easy for either one of us. I so wanted to be a comfort to her, but I cannot live her life and she cannot live mine. We’ve been traveling companions since I was born, but now we seem to be getting in each other’s way. Perhaps the anger we feel will make the final letting-go easier.

# MY TRAIN WRECK

*March 2005*

TODAY THE CASHIER AT THE GROCERY STORE MADE the simple mistake of packing one of my bags the wrong way. I let her know it in no uncertain terms. "You just placed four cans of tomatoes and a box of detergent on top of the lettuce. Hasn't anyone here ever taught you how to pack groceries?" I'm sure it wasn't just the words I used that made her shrivel; it was my tone of voice and the way I glared at her that made her look as though I had slapped her face. Catching myself, I wanted to cry. I wanted to get down on the floor and grovel. I was a raging bitch. Out of control!

At home, I try not to let on that I'm on fire inside. But whenever I leave the house, I'm armed for a fight. Should a driver cut me off or be too slow to move when the light turns green, the horn on my car becomes my mouthpiece, letting the world know how I'm feeling. I'm being far more than assertive; I'm overly aggressive and blaming strangers on the street for my suffering.

It doesn't occur to me to ask myself why I'm so angry and why I need to take it out on anyone who looks at me cross-eyed.

The only place I've felt some solace is in my studio in town. I've been there every day this week, packing it up. Tomorrow I'll be moving all of it to my new studio at home, where I'll undoubtedly be interrupted often. In town, I've been completely alone, without the phone ringing or Mom asking me to do something for her.

Though I'm no longer interested in trying to show or sell my work, I'm still an artist and need peace and quiet to create. I'm not interested in doing any more photography at the moment, nor am I drawn to painting. What does get my creative juices flowing is making small collages in my journal, from torn bits of paper, found objects, and words cut from magazines, which usually express my feelings in short, poetic bursts. One afternoon, I picked up a copy of *Art Papers* magazine and saw a headline on its cover. I cut it out immediately. It was the perfect quote for my day: "One is unavoidably faithful to the dead body growing inside one."

I write in another journal every day about the river just outside my door at home and the ways in which its flow figures into the lives of those who live along its banks, including a variety of geese, ducks, deer, wild turkeys, foxes, raccoons, and me. It's my daily check-in on the natural world I so love. The way the Canada geese gather together in an armada of sorts on summer evenings and paddle their way down the river fascinates me. There are red-winged blackbirds that nest in the shrubs and reeds along the shore, and occasionally I can hear the plaintive calls of loons when they stop overnight on the river. Rereading my most recent writings, I'm inspired to gather them together into a book of essays, poems, and photographs inspired by the seasonal changes that go on around me. I place the idea at the top of my intention list. It's projects like this one that I hope will keep me sane as life continues to get more complicated.

Bill and I are constantly arguing about silly things, like who should be cleaning up the dog poop in the yard. We have a good marriage, but Mom's presence, my state of mind, and my behavior are interfering with it. If we shout at each other, Mom can hear every word. I miss my privacy and feel uncomfortable with our bed being positioned just above her living room, where she spends most of her time. During the renovation, we neglected to put proper sound insulation between our floors and the ceilings in Mom's apartment, but we're not about to start tearing things apart again now.

Mom is always looking over my shoulder. I don't like being watched. When I go out and work in the garden, she tells me what to plant and how to do it. She thinks I've never planted a garden before. After observing my way of juggling too many projects and my obviously frustrated state of mind, she tells me, "Your life is a train wreck—out of control and ready to destroy everything in its path." My retort—"I have a life of my own, with my own needs to fill, and my own way of doing things"—makes no difference. With Mom, there is no winning, and I'm too tired to fight. I lick my wounds in silence, knowing she will never understand how I feel.

Still, I need to come to terms with Mom's presence and everything else that is overwhelming me. I do need to slow down and "simplify" my life, but I have no real idea what that means. I've been keeping myself overly busy so that I won't hear the chatter in my head, but when I try to keep myself in check, my anger only gets bolder and eventually spills over into everyone else's space.

Taking a break from the chaos I'm up to my ears in, I go to dinner with a friend who is just starting a jewelry-making business. She shows me some of the lovely beaded necklaces and earrings she makes. I don't wear much jewelry, but I can see how a necklace of gorgeous amber, coral, and turquoise beads just might make a difference in the way I'm feeling. She encourages me to start a beading project.

Off I go the next day to the local bead shop, where a new addiction will soon have me in its clutches. I have never seen so many beads in all my life: tiny seed beads in breathtaking colors from Czechoslovakia, large, hand-blown glass beads from Italy, and semiprecious stones from around the world—quartz, amethyst, tourmaline, and agate. I purchase several that catch my fancy and sign up for a day-long bead-stringing class, to be held the following week.

Ten classes in a variety of beading techniques later, I can't get enough of it. All I want to do is buy and use beads to make jewelry. And then I fall head over heels with life-size French beaded flowers. I *must* learn how to make those as well. My checkbook is barely maintaining the amount I keep stashed away for a rainy day, my brilliant idea of writing a book about life on the river begins to dim, and I don't have time for the poetry group I've always loved attending. I know I'm in trouble—I'm overdosing in a huge way, and I'm anxious about the amount of money I'm spending on beading tools and supplies—but I continue to sign up for whatever class is being offered next.

The beads are my medicine. What alcohol does for Mom,

beads do for me. They go everywhere with me. I bead on road trips, while Bill drives. I bead in doctor's offices, on planes, and in hotel rooms. They work better at keeping me happy than the knitting binge I went on a couple of years ago. I'm frustrated that there isn't enough time for me to make all the jewelry I have in mind. I sometimes let my daily workout routine slide to make more time for this new love, and more than once I've been close to tears when I had to stop working on a project because I had to prepare dinner.

My already-huge garden, another addiction/obsession, vies for my attention. It's spring, and I want to add color to the flowerbeds that have only shrubs and ornamental grasses tucked here and there. The azaleas are just about done blooming, and I envision planting perennials that will shock the green dullness with bright colors: pink and orange Echinacea, bright yellow black-eyed Susans, lilies in red and gold. When I visit local garden centers, my interests expand to the many other plants I am not so familiar with. I want them all.

I also believe that I should be putting in time writing that book about the river. I want to see friends, and I need to start up my healthy exercise routine again. At night I fall into bed in tears. I don't have time for all of it. The idea of simplicity is a sham. There are too many plants to put in the ground, and too many beading projects I want to learn about. My bones and muscles are sore from the bending and the contortions I put them through in order to get my yard work done. The endless daily chores, like laundry and cooking, only add to my frustration. And then there is Mom.

Maybe she's right about my life being a "train wreck." I am overwhelmed, but I keep it to myself.

# AND THEN ...

*Summer 2005*

ANOTHER YEAR HAS COME AND GONE. MOM IS eighty-two now, and her memory continues to diminish. She's unable to balance her checkbook. She complains about it on a daily basis. I volunteer to help, but she says, "No, I want to do it myself." It's hard for her to accept that her mind isn't as sharp as it used to be. She doesn't believe that some of the inevitable things that happen to the aging population could happen to her as well. I can't say I blame her when I notice my own growing forgetfulness. When Mom first moved to Virginia, I suggested she join the very active senior center in town. She gave it a whirl, but after a bus trip to visit several museums in Washington, DC, she declared she didn't like hanging out with "old people." She still seems to believe she will live forever.

We bump into and bruise each other on a daily basis.

When I share my woes with a friend, she says, "If it's not one thing, it's your mother." It's funny for the moment, but truer words were never spoken.

One afternoon, after hours of obvious frustration, she comes to me, throws her checkbook onto the kitchen table, and says, "Okay, I give up. See if you can figure it out." That evening, I sit down to untangle the mess. She's made addition and subtraction mistakes, and in the end the bank claims there is a total of $500 more in her account than what her checkbook shows. I take a break and go over it again. My figures are correct. The next morning, when I show her the extra funds the bank claims she has, she remembers that she deposited $500 into the account but had never added it to her checkbook balance. "I just wanted the extra money there so that if I overdraw my account the bad checks will be covered." What can I say? For someone who is forgetful, maybe that makes sense. Now I balance her checkbook on a monthly basis, correcting her mistakes, knowing there are extra funds she doesn't want to show.

In late July, I take her to the doctor for a checkup. Her cough is getting worse. He orders up a chest X-ray to see what's going on in her lungs. He asks if she is still smoking. Knowing I'll tell the truth if she doesn't, she looks at me, hesitates, then finally confesses, "Yes, just a little bit."

A day or two later, she gets a call requesting that she return to the doctor's office as soon as possible. I know that's not a good sign. I begin creating stories in my head, diagnosing the problem and what the outcome will be. None of them has a happy ending. I ask Mom what she thinks, but she has nothing to say except, "I'm not ready to kick the bucket." That's the only term she uses when referring to death or dying. I always thought she was just being a comedian and always laughed when she said it. But now it's not so funny.

I have trouble sleeping the night before we return to Dr. Hamner's office. Big questions fill the night. How will I handle what I think is coming? More importantly, how will Mom handle it? Will I be able to stay strong for her and truly help, or will I fall apart as the stress mounts? Will she have a good death, versus one filled with hatred and fear? I'm someone who often makes the smallest problems into life-shattering catastrophes, and the tangled sheets and blanket on my bed hint at where my mind has been.

The next morning, the doctor tells us that there are several spots on Mom's lungs and recommends she see an oncologist. Despite my intuitive knowing, I'm numb. I have a billion questions to ask, but the doctor says he can't give me any answers. I'll just have to wait to talk to the oncologist. Mom has a faint smile on her face and seems somehow untouched by the news. She has a lot to think about and big decisions to make. It's impossible to know exactly what she's feeling.

The first appointment with Dr. Packard is brief and to the point. Before anything is certain, Mom needs to have a biopsy and an MRI. Getting her on the schedule will take a few days. I'm not good at waiting. I have difficulty focusing on anything, including my beading. I've been working on the French beaded lilies, but now they sit unnoticed as I count the days until we know something more. Mom's earlier smile has faded, and she, too, is anxious to know the results of those procedures. I try to engage her in conversation about what she is feeling, but she won't tell me anything other than, "Whatever it is, I'm going to fight it."

I call my brothers to let them know what's up. They don't say much. Neither of them has been here to visit Mom since last summer, and they aren't in a rush to come now. What is wrong with this family? Both Mom and I have been helping them pay their bills from time to time, and we're actually supporting one of them, who has ADD and is unable to work. Where is their compassion and appreciation for their mother? I agree we have major family issues, but just once, can't we come together at a time when Mom could use their love and support? I know that whatever is coming will land squarely on Bill's and my shoulders.

The biopsy and MRI confirm stage four cancer in both lungs, but there's no sign of it anywhere else. The doctor talks to us about chemo, and then we visit the radiologist, who gives us the rundown on how that will work, should Mom decide to go in that direction. Everyone is clear and honest, and they give her two options to think about.

Option one: She could do nothing and just live with what lies ahead. That would probably give her the shortest life expectancy, but she'd be free from nausea, constant exhaustion, and the other side effects of pumping poisons into her body. When and if the pain got unbearable, it would be managed with morphine. Option two: She could do chemo, radiation, or both and could expect to have about two years to live, but with all of the consequences those treatments bring.

We're told that her current problem with emphysema isn't helping the situation. When Mom is asked whether she has any questions, she answers, "No. I just want to get rid of the cancer." They ask again if she is still smoking. Her answer, as expected, is a very grumpy no. When I tell them the truth, she gives me an icy look and they tell her, "No amount of chemo or radiation is going to help if you don't stop. You need to be totally honest with us about what you are willing to do." Interested in her quality of life and knowing she'll never quit smoking, I secretly hope she'll choose the first option and live out her days without treatment. But she chooses both radiation and chemo. I'm disheartened, but it's her body and her life, and no one has the right to intrude on another person's choices.

A day later, it's decided that because some of the cancer is very close to her esophagus, radiation is inappropriate. It would make swallowing difficult or impossible if the esophagus is burned during treatment. Disappointed, but impatient to get started, Mom wants to go ahead with chemo. I'm not sure she really understands what is going to happen to her. She doesn't ask any questions and seems a bit fuzzy about it. Bill and I try to explain the procedures, help her set up her appointments, and cheer her on.

Throughout the early weeks of chemo, Bill is his usual calm and collected self. He drives Mom back and forth to chemo. I, for some reason, take on the role of an overly enthusiastic cheerleader. I'm hyper, crack jokes, laugh a lot, especially in public, and have a smile etched on my face that gets more and more painful every day. I'm living on adrenaline and feel like crap. I don't recognize who I've become.

Mom, on the other hand, seems unfazed at first but then begins looking sad. The chemo is stealing her energy, and she's on guard waiting for her hair to start falling out. She sleeps endlessly in front of the TV. For her it's just another presence in the room. I supply her with mystery novels, which she usually loves to read, but they sit unopened. She is slowly taking in what is happening to her. When I ask if she's afraid of what's ahead, she answers, "No," without further comment. But the expression on her face leads me to believe otherwise.

Building up my courage, I gently tell her, "Mom, I think it's time for you to give me your driver's license and car keys. Chemo fog is sure to start soon."

She says sadly, "Okay, but let me have one more drive to the grocery store by myself." When it takes her a long time to return, I begin worrying that she's had an accident or maybe even run away. But in reality I think she's simply driving around town, enjoying the feel of the steering wheel in her hands and feeling the power of being in charge of her own life. Two hours later, she returns, hands me her keys, and says nothing. I feel her pain. Her last bastion of freedom is gone.

## LIVING *with* CANCER

*September 2006*

ALL OF MY RELATIVES WHO ARE NO LONGER LIVING succumbed to cancer. I know that one day, when I'm not looking, it will be back in my life. It is not welcome here. But there is nothing I can do. It has a mind of its own and goes where it chooses, eating away the bodies of those it selects, until there is nothing left. In turn, this greedy intruder dies with its prey, because there is nothing left to nourish it. I thank God that I have not fallen victim to it . . . yet.

But it seems one step closer as it assaults my mother, the woman who gave me life. When my cholesterol levels were first checked years ago and found to be high, my doctor told me to start taking statins in order to lower my bad cholesterol levels and prevent a heart attack. I tried it, but all it did was cause major aches and pains that went away shortly after I stopped taking it. When I informed him that I wouldn't take it any more, he chided, "You're putting yourself at great risk." But I reminded him, "There is no history of heart disease in my family. My relatives have all died of cancer." He nodded and agreed that cancer will most likely take me down one day, unless a dump truck comes my way first.

So here we are, dealing with the big C. It's here in my house, instead of next door, halfway around the country or the world. As usual, when bad things happen, I rise to the occasion, like the time my brother Zed called to tell us he'd fallen and broken his hip and was in the hospital in Burlington, Vermont, about to undergo surgery. Mom panicked and I took over, long-distance from Virginia, talking to the chaplain at the hospital, who happened to be Zed's friend. He helped us sort out all of the financial ins and outs and found another friend with whom Zed could stay when he first got out of the hospital and was unable to move around. He also found Zed a new apartment, where he'd have the services of an elevator when he did go home. When I'm first at the scene of a family disaster, I'm good at telling everyone what to do and whom to call, as well as devising several plans in case one fails. I considered going up to Vermont myself to make sure that everything was running smoothly, but at the last minute, I stayed home, knowing I couldn't do any more than I already had. My behavior in this cancer calamity is no exception.

There are consequences for my sometimes-bossy ways, though. When I tell Mom what she should be doing in order to take care of herself, she often growls, "Yes, Mother," bringing on her inner child, who will have none of my maternal words. I'm uncomfortable taking on the role of the parent yet I feel as if I have no choice, since Mom isn't doing much to keep herself well. I'm brave, refusing to give in to the disease that is knocking all of us apart with sadness and grief. Bill is philosophical. Mom hides in a haze of depression one minute and then, without warning, comes out roaring like a lion ready to kill whoever is in her way. That's often me.

When I suggest to Mom's doctor that she's depressed, he prescribes an antidepressant. Mom has a fit, denying that she's feeling low. She tells the doctor, "Miss Shrink here doesn't know what the hell she's talking about. I'm perfectly happy; I just want everyone to leave me alone." He tells her to take it anyway. Mom gives in, adding one more pill to her growing medicine chest. She's got pills for just about everything, like constipation, and some of the other side effects of chemo. There are also pills to take care of the side effects of all the other pills. It's an indescribable look into what those with cancer go through when they choose to treat it. Sadly, I have to admit that this is not part of the script I pay much attention to. I'm already giving too much of myself in the effort to keep Mom's health intact. I don't think I can keep track of one more thing for her.

One of us takes Mom to the hospital, where she undergoes chemo every other week. She spends most of the day hooked up to an IV that pumps supposedly cancer-eradicating poison into her body. The problem is that it also damages healthy cells. She comes home feeling drained. She has frequent headaches, doesn't eat much, and seems to be growing skinnier by the day. Her earlier memory difficulties are exacerbated by "chemo brain," which causes additional problems with her cognitive skills. She's also weak, and her balance is off, adding the possibility of falling and further injury to her already over-stressed body.

The house is filled with unending worry, so, during a two-week span between chemo treatments six and seven, Bill and I throw restraint out the door and plan a trip to the beach for a week to rest and rejuvenate. I find two highly recommended nurses to come in and look after Mom while we're gone. They will prepare her meals, run errands, and take care of all of her needs. I instruct them that they don't need to spend every minute with her and that they can go upstairs to my part of the house when she doesn't need them. But they'll check in with her frequently and be alert to whatever she requires. I warn them that Mom is a very private person and can be extremely difficult. They assure me that they can handle it. They suggest that they give Mom a whistle she can blow to get their attention. Mom says, "I like that idea."

When I introduce them to my mother, she's extremely pleasant and welcoming. I'm quite surprised, since, at her last checkup, she complained to the doctor, "They [Bill and I] are always going away on vacation and leaving me behind." The part about our always being on vacation is untrue, but sometimes we do need to get away from her and to find some peace. These days especially, I need to remember what life is like without her constant presence.

On the day we plan to leave, we shuttle the dogs and cats off to their caretaker, pack up the car, and breathe huge sighs of relief, leaving Mom and everything else behind.

Just three miles down the road, Bill exclaims, "I can't believe we're actually doing this. Let's hope no emergencies arise."

I laugh, responding, "We just won't answer the phone if it rings. Let's pretend we're running away and will never have to go back." It sounds like a great idea, but we both know better.

Five hours later, on an exquisite fall day, we arrive on the Outer Banks of North Carolina, feeling free at last. It's sunny and warm, and the surf in front of our rental home is already soothing my weary brain. I pray we'll be able to stay for the entire week without having to rush back home to Mom.

For the first time in what seems like a century, we're alone together, breathing deeply and grateful for this gift of time and space. We've brought along a few DVDs and books, but mostly we just want to sit and stare at the ocean. I have a few beading projects that I've neglected and plan to walk the beach every day, collecting shells and watching ducks and geese fly by on their way to warmer climes for the winter. Being out in the natural world in a season when there are few other people about is refreshing and relaxing. Most of the time, I am either alone or one of a handful of people walking the shore. We sleep in every day, stay up late watching the stars, and fall asleep to the sound of the ocean hurling itself against the shore.

Two days later, the phone rings. It's one of the nurses looking after Mom. "Your mother fired us today. What do you want us to do?" I tell her in no uncertain terms that she is *not* fired and to stay the course. I call my mother and tell her that her decision to fire them is not an option. We argue. Mom says, "I don't want those women hanging around and staring at me." She complains about the food they've prepared for her, even though she instructs them what to make and how to do it. I'm pissed as hell and let her know it. "You can't fire the nurses. I'm paying them, not you. I need a break. They will be there every day whether you like it or not. I am not returning home until the end of the week, and if you want to be a problem, fine. But I'm not coming back just because you don't like having them around."

She's a bit taken aback by my sudden fury. Some might call what I've just done "tough love," but right now what I'm feeling is more like tough hate. Whenever I try to give myself some personal care, Mom usually gets in the way. I spend the rest of the day and evening pissing and moaning about my fate. "Why must I have a mother like her, and why don't I just put her in a nursing home and forget about her?" Bill feels the same way. It's his getaway, too, and taking care of my mother is no fun for him, either. But, always filled with words of wisdom, he says, "Because she's your mother and you love her. You don't ever get to choose your family members. It's just what you're given."

The morning after Mom calls, I rise early and sit on the beach to meditate as the sun begins to rise. The crashing and booming of yesterday's sea have given way to a smooth and glassy surface. A small flock of sanderlings follow the gentle waves back and forth, foraging for special treats the waves wash up on the sand. They snatch up the goodies, then race back up the shore, just out of reach of the next incoming wave.

In the early-morning light, I realize that one of the things that keeps me going is my insight meditation group at home in Charlottesville. I've grown very interested in Buddhism and often attend the group's Tuesday night meditation meetings. I've been drawn to this group of people for their ease and simple approach to life. There is no dogma, no angry god to be constantly leery of, only the wish to live gently, with compassion for our fellow sufferers. Everyone I've met there is friendly and very caring. We meditate as a group for about forty-five minutes, then have a ten-minute break to socialize and use the facilities. Afterward, we sit down again and the teacher in charge for the evening gives a talk about some aspect of meditation and Buddhist philosophy. Most evenings I feel as though the teacher is talking directly to me. I know everyone in the room feels the same way. We're all suffering in one way or another and are seeking a way to be more comfortable in the messes we find ourselves in. Their company and the commonality in this extraordinary community comfort me.

I've spent many evenings reading through books by contemporary Buddhist teachers to find a way to make peace with my mother. They all say that the difficult people in our lives are our teachers. They give us insights into our own suffering. Often when I react to Mom, I realize that I'm seeing my own behavior in her. She's my mirror. I try to ignore what I see and, in disgust, blame her for whatever is happening, filling my own mind with self-hatred and fear. It's a long, hard process. How can I accept things as they are? I realize that rather than running away from my discomfort, I need to sit with it and listen to it speak. It's easier said than done, but I keep trying to move forward, despite my frequent backsliding. Within my meditation practice, I look for and find hope that one day I'll find a path to my own happiness.

We hear nothing more from Mom or the nurses for the rest of the week. We head home feeling refreshed and ready to take on whatever the future holds. It's not knowing what will happen next that grabs at my nerves. Having this time to just be, with Bill or myself, as I walk the beach alone, has allowed me to steep in the individual moments of each day without the strain of being constantly on call. Though I'm relaxed now, I know the stress will be back. But if I can continue to care for myself in the same way I try to care for my mother, I believe I can make it through whatever lies ahead. Bill's final words before we walk back through our front door sums up my own feelings: "Life is good and worth living."

## FINDING COMMON GROUND

*November 2006*

DURING MY WEEK AT THE BEACH, I GAVE A LOT OF thought to my relationship with Mom. When I invited her to live with us, I had expectations that I now realize were more than either one of us could live with. I created a fantasy in which Mom and I would reconnect, making our time living together a healing event in which we would support each other through the coming trials of life. It was one of my "perfect family" scenarios, in which mother and daughter come together after years of injuring each other to find peace and common ground as the mother slips toward death. Delusional at best, it was a wish-upon-a-star idea, like the pony I knew I'd win in a contest by sending in the "perfect" name. I was eight years old and absolutely positive that the palomino pony would be mine when I sent the best name in the world, Star. I decided on that name because at the top of the blaze on its face was a perfectly shaped white star. I was heartbroken when it was announced that another girl, who lived in New Jersey, had become the proud owner of the pony that was meant to be the love of my life. I was mad and had a tantrum, and when I ranted about it, Mom simply smiled and said, "We don't get all the things in life that we want." When I finally did get a Shetland pony for my kids when they were small, he turned out to be a nasty boy who reared up and threw them off every time they climbed up on his back. He didn't last long in our barn. As I remember that time, it's quite apparent that, as I grow into my sixties, perhaps it's time to release some of my childish dreams.

Still, it's hard. Is it really childish to want to rebuild the bond with the woman who birthed me? We spent the first twenty or so years of my life living together. There must be more than the fact that she's my mother that holds us together. I need to explore the makeup of the glue that's kept us cemented together over the years. I want to find commonality with her, gain a new understanding of and tolerance for the mystery woman who lives with me now and who, at times, makes my life insufferable.

Mom once confessed to me that when she was quite young she wanted to be a nun. She never said why. I suspect it was because she thought it would allow her to escape from the extremely abusive family situation she was living in. Like Mom, I've frequently felt the pull of a monastic life for that same reason.

As a highly sensitive child, I dreamed of a place where I could find respite from everyday stress. The constant strain of being the oldest and needing to be the perfect daughter was exhausting. My parents' ceaseless battles and my assigned role as the messenger between them made me fearful and anxious. I felt the anger in their hostile words and absorbed the shock waves. "Joan, tell your father that dinner is on the table, now," and, "Tell her I'll be there when I'm damn ready," were messages that displeased both of them, leaving me in the middle of a war that had nothing to do with me.

It must have been the same for Mom when she was small, hearing the relentless sounds of exploding grenades that her parents threw at each other. It's not a comforting way to grow up. Neither one of us had any idea that those ceaseless clashes would follow us into adulthood and color the way we react to the world around us.

A short-lived but painful bit of experience with the Catholic Church and formal religion came when I was quite young, leaving me feeling as if there was no place to find ease from life's struggles. Catholics but not churchgoers, my parents took it upon themselves to make sure that I was educated and knew about God, Jesus, and all the saints. When I was seven, they sent me to what the church called Religious Instruction. I had envisioned Heaven to be a like a huge garden, filled with flowers, birds, and bees, where love was doled out without end. I believed Hell to be a hot and sweaty place where one stood shoveling coal into a huge furnace, making the place even hotter. I wanted to go to Heaven, not Hell. But when I started learning the "rules" from scowling, knuckle-rapping nuns, as they prepared me for my First Holy Communion, any interest I had in learning more about either Heaven or Hell flew out the window. The only thing that interested me was getting my own string of rosary beads, a pretty white dress, and a veil to wear for that "special" occasion.

After three classes, I wanted out when a nun whacked a classmate's hands with a ruler for not paying attention and being unable to answer a question. Hearing my friend scream and seeing her tears, I became afraid that I would be next. I had to be constantly on guard to make sure that I would be spared a painful punishment. I took no more imaginative trips in my head when I was bored, and by the end of each class my body was stiff and ached from being constantly at attention.

The more classes I attended, the more afraid I became. Those dreary women dressed in black and white wore heavy crosses around their necks, rarely smiled, and were fixated on getting their religious messages across. I wondered if they had hair underneath their head coverings, imagining it to be limp and greasy. The only human parts that were ever visible were their ashen faces and crinkly hands, always wrapped in rosary beads.

Because I was a literalist, when I was told that the money collected at Mass every Sunday went to God, I envisioned quarters, nickels, and even dollar bills sprouting wings and rising up into the heavens. I wondered what happened once it got there. What would you need to buy in Heaven? I thought everything one needed would be provided.

What terrified me most was discovering that children and adults who were never baptized would not be allowed to go to Heaven. Instead, they would be sent to Limbo, never receiving the benefits of "the one glorious God." Even at my tender age, I was sure I didn't want to be a member of that kind of church. Why would God do something like that? In my young mind's eye, I saw Limbo as a place where newborn babies lay on the ground without blankets to keep them warm and old people were dressed in clothes that were beginning to fray. All of them were hungry. When I asked my mother about it, she didn't have any answers. "That's just the way it is," she said, shrugging her shoulders. She was no help, and it wasn't until I got older and began inventing my own "religion" that I was able to find comfort in the words "God," "holy," and "sacred."

The need to go to confession every week inside a small, closet-like box—to tell a strange man, whose face I could not see and whom I had never met, all the things I had done wrong also disturbed me. I would never admit a wrongdoing to my father, so how could I tell a man I didn't know or trust any of my secrets?

I didn't completely understand what sins were anyway, and on the occasions when I was forced to go to confession, I often made up things to satisfy what I thought the requirements were. I knew that lying was bad, but was telling a white lie to make someone feel better a sin? Was hitting my brothers because I'd been blamed for something they'd done a sin? I had a feeling that my hatred of having to go to confession would definitely be called a sin. I was confused. Where was the love that God was supposed to bring to us? Who would bring food to the babies and old people in Limbo? So it often was that when the priest would ask, "Tell me about your sins," I would have no words.

Afterward, kneeling in a pew and doing penance, I wondered if the prayers I was told to say would make a difference or not. To be on the safe side, I kept repeating, "I'm sorry, I'm really sorry," for all of the horrific things that I hadn't really done. I didn't know that later, as an adult, I would continue to say those words in everyday life, to apologize for silly things I did that offended no one.

The final blow that kept me from going to church for good came a few years later. It began in 1942, when my parents fell in love and married the night before my dad was shipped off to fight the Nazis in Europe. To make things quick and simple, they drove from New York to Elkton, Maryland, where they became man and wife before a justice of the peace.

When I was born, I was baptized immediately. But ten years later, when Mom and Dad finally got around to thinking about having my brothers baptized, things were different. While my parents were consulting a priest about the ceremony, he discovered that they had not been married in a church. He said, "I won't baptize Reid and Zed, because in God's eyes you are living in sin." He also called my brothers and me bastards for the same reason.

Shamed and infuriated, my parents never went inside a Catholic church again, unless it was for a wedding or a funeral. My mother, whose family members were devout Catholics, must have felt terribly degraded, losing what little faith she might have had in a just and caring God.

The church's rejection shook me to the core. My brothers and I would go to Limbo instead of Heaven. I believed that the church had taken on the role of abuser to all of us. God—who I had been led to believe was the world's hero, the force that always protected everyone—was no longer there for me. He didn't recognize my family members or me as worthy souls. He'd simply ditched us on the side of the road.

I watched my mother come to terms with the rejection from the church. She would never admit to living in sin or having children who were bastards. She and my father were legally married, and if the church couldn't accept that fact and the children that resulted from that union, they could go roast in hell.

I followed in her footsteps as she created a path for herself in the great outdoors, calling the forest her cathedral and believing in a simpler God, who lived among the trees and the creatures that found their place in the natural world. It wasn't a place continually filled with love and laughter. Bad things happened on the forest floor. The sight of a fox killing a baby rabbit is never a happy occasion. But it's real, a fact, that in order for some to live, others must die. We as humans are but a small piece in the enormous mystery of the universe. We are all one, and we all have a purpose.

This is the common ground I have shared with my mother. I find it sad that we have both lost our way amid the tangle of right and wrong, love and hate, living and dying. I know that I will find that path again, but it isn't possible to bring Mom with me unless she chooses to come along. She walks a different way now, and I will not follow.

# WAITING

*January 2006*

I'VE NEVER BEEN THIS CLOSELY INTERTWINED WITH someone who has cancer, or been so close to the process of human dying. Unlike our beloved cats and dogs, we must endure our pain and disease until we are in a vegetative state or we simply stop breathing on our own. When we decide we've had enough, our physicians cannot help us to cut the cord of life. We are held prisoners in our failing bodies, being fed tasteless but nourishing liquids that are pumped directly into our veins day after day. And when we can no longer breathe adequately, our lungs are kept inflated by machines dispensing oxygen until another machine we're plugged into tells our caretakers that our brains are no longer functioning. Then we are allowed to die.

Mom isn't close to dying at the moment, yet my heart hurts as I watch her struggle with her disease and failing brain. She is extremely vulnerable and unable to hide it. She is bald now and wears a short, blond wig that makes her look like someone trying to be half her age. All she needs is some mascara and fire-engine-red lipstick, and she'd look like a failing lady of the night. She looks better with a scarf over her head, and without any head covering at all, she's stunningly beautiful. However, she's ashamed to let the whole world know that she has cancer and that in a year or two she'll most likely be dead. She treats the cancer as if it's revenge for some crime she's committed. She doesn't seem to understand that most people will face cancer in their lifetime, whether it's their own or a loved one's.

As for me, I'm not terribly inspired by anything these days. Small beading projects are easy to carry along on Mom's doctor and hospital visits when I know there will be a lot of waiting around. I've begun a number of projects, growing bored with each one and then starting another that looks more exciting. As a result, numerous half-finished projects fill the shelves in my studio.

Mom is no longer doing chemo. The doctor wants to wait a while to see how she does without it. There will be scans scheduled in the coming weeks and months to see if the cancer has retreated, grown, or metastasized. We're stuck, sitting on our hands while the rest of the world moves forward.

We humans are always waiting and watching the clock. We never have a clue about what will happen next, so why can't we just move through the sticky parts and enjoy all the moments that we do have? We wait to grow up. We wait for the love of our life to come along and sweep us off our feet. We wait for the other shoe to drop, or for the rain to stop so that we can go out and play. We wait for payday, Santa Claus, the Easter

Bunny, the Tooth Fairy, and the right time to follow our dreams. We're never satisfied or happy with the status quo. Too often we complain, "If only," wondering why things aren't different and why we have no momentum in our lives.

Just before Christmas, Hannah, my cat, had a stroke while she was sitting in my lap. It was nine o'clock at night. She suddenly had a seizure that told me that she was near the end. Her bladder let go, and she meowed softly as her body functions started closing down. She'd been diagnosed with congestive heart failure a few months earlier, but at the time she looked great and wasn't suffering. The vet said that she'd probably be fine for a while and that there would be no mistaking when it was time to let her go. Up until this stroke, I had enjoyed watching her live her life with gusto, hunting for the voles that drove her crazy and enjoying her naps in the sun's warmth on the living room sofa.

I wrapped her in a towel and drove her to the emergency vet, holding her in my lap with one hand while steering with the other. The doctor agreed it was time. I held her tight while he injected her with a sleep potion. I said good-bye and let her go. A week later, I scattered her ashes under the apple trees in our yard. I rued the moments I'd missed with her while I waited for some news about my mother's health.

Dogs and cats have always been my best friends and as important to me as my human family. When I was a small child, I wanted a cat, but my father hated them. There were always dogs in my life, and they were my comfort when life was difficult, my parents were fighting, or I had done something wrong and was being punished. They licked away my tears when I knew nobody else loved me, and they never told me that I wasn't any good. There was Booby, Prince, Morgan, Gretchen, and so many others. All of them helped me to move through my troubles and feel loved.

After I was married, I finally got a cat. Nikki, a dark gray-and-white beauty, came from one of Bill's students, whose father said he would drown the kittens living out in his barn if she couldn't find homes for them. We decided we could at least save one. Nikki adored Derry, our first dog, who would gently pick Nikki up with her mouth and carry her around the house.

Though death is always nearby, I usually don't give it a second thought. But here at home, with Mom losing weight quickly, I'm reminded every day that it's closer than I think. I ponder my own demise, seeing my face in place of my mother's. The days are long and filled with dark clouds that threaten the sun. With my studio now here at home, I can no longer escape downtown for a few hours to be by myself.

Missing Hannah badly, I decide to volunteer at our local SPCA to help take care of the numerous cats that are up for adoption. It'll get me out of the house and away from Mom for a little while. And I'll be able to have some cat cuddling time, which I long for.

I'm assigned to our local PetSmart, which generously provides space to the SPCA for cats and kittens that are in need of forever homes. I'm to arrive every Monday morning before the store opens, clean out litter boxes, feed and play with the kitties, and be ready to meet folks looking for a new companion. At eleven-thirty, another volunteer will come in to take my place.

It goes well at first. I'm glad for the break from my regular routine and love being with these purring balls of fur. All kinds of cats—some adult cats, but mostly kittens—come and go to new homes, but never on my shift. I'm alarmed that several have been here for over six months. I try to give them extra time out of their cages and as much love as I can. I figure out that the morning shift is the quietest time for adoptions. Most of the action occurs in the afternoons and evenings, when kids are out of school and families have time to come in to find a new pet. I request a shift later in the day, but no one wants to trade places with me, and I'm told, "You're needed where you are."

I keep at it for another month and suddenly wake up to the fact that I am still playing caregiver, adding needy cats as my newest patients. And I'm not reaping the rewards of seeing these elegant creatures go to new homes. I took this on because I needed some sunshine in my life, not smelly litter boxes or watching the clock for someone to come along and adopt an animal companion. I sit and wait. I feel useless. Deep sadness and depression still fill my days. I don't want to wait any longer.

When I announce that I can no longer be a volunteer, I'm stormed with various versions of "Why not? Please stay" and "We need you." The director of volunteers knows my situation but doesn't understand. She argues with me and cajoles me: "This is the perfect opportunity to get away from your sick mother. You know we need you, too."

Before the two weeks I've given them to replace me are up, I decide to take home one of the longest-caged residents. She is a young, sleek, black-and-white tuxedo cat, full of energy and in desperate need of freedom. Her eyes are an intense yellow, and her small pink nose softens her fierce look. Whenever I pass by her cage, she swats at me to get my attention. When I stop and talk with her, she butts her head against my hand as I rub her ears and chin. She gives me gentle love nips. I fully understand what she wants. As I remove her from her cage to take her home, I imagine myself being set free.

On my last day at PetSmart, I fill in for someone who can't cover their regular shift in the afternoon. A family of five comes in to look for a cat to take home. The three kids are noisy and try opening the cages without my permission. When I allow them to pet a few of the cats, they squeeze and grab at them. They can't seem to hear me when I tell them to stop. I'd like to twist an ear or two and banish these brats from the store. When they show interest in one of my favorites, who has been in the same cage for over six months, I tell them that she is being held until her new owner can come and pick her up.

It's a lie. Peppermint is a quiet, laid-back ginger cat who loves to be held, but I know she won't do well being squeezed and assaulted by a bunch of badly behaved children. My lie enables me to rescue one more cat; I buy another crate and take her with me when I leave. Bill is not happy. As I try to fall asleep that night, my mind rattles on and keeps returning to what Bill said when I walked in the door that afternoon with another rescue. "Don't we have enough to take care of around here? Do we really need something more?" He slammed the door and went to his office.

I'm a rescuer, just like my mother. Like her, I cannot stand to watch animals suffering. I also try to rescue people. I know I've been trying to rescue my mother, but I'm not doing such a great job. Right now, everything feels out of control. I'm stumbling in the dark, down a long, lonely road, in a strange land where no one speaks my language. Sobbing, I think, *I need someone to rescue me!*

# HELP

*May 2006*

MOM SPENDS HER DAYS IN FRONT OF THE TELEVISION and rarely has anything positive to say. I drive her to appointments, try to prepare appetizing meals for her, and am on call all day long. I rarely go anywhere, unless Bill is home. I worry she'll get tangled up in her oxygen line or blow the place up when she lights a cigarette. Yes, she's still smoking, and though she tries to hide it, I invariably catch her. The harsh smell of cigarette smoke is always the giveaway. She has trouble climbing the stairs to our level of the house, yet refuses to use the chairlift that is there just for her. If I make a reasonable suggestion about something that might help her feel better, she cuts me off and says, "Mind your own damn business." She won't tell me how she is feeling, either physically or emotionally, though I can usually tell by the way she looks and responds. It's a no-win situation for both of us. Being a caretaker is a sticky, thankless job.

I don't believe I'd ever hit my mother, but being cruel in response to her outbursts is certainly not above me. We disagree about things like clothing styles, and she never hesitates to tell me things like, "That's a stupid-looking sweater. Why did you buy that?" "This sweater is for young people like me, not for old ladies," might be my response. We miss the potential humor in our words by taking things far too personally.

When it comes to the garden, she insists that the soil here in Virginia is not good for growing anything because it's not the rich, dark loam she's used to working with in Vermont. While I agree that Vermont soil is much richer, I have a hard time convincing her that the plants in my garden here in Virginia are growing beautifully and are just as healthy as those growing up north. It's an unending contest in which each of us tries to prove ourself right and the other wrong. I'm very much aware when it's happening, but I don't know how to stop myself. Am I supposed to agree that the sky is purple? As a small child, I believed everything Mom told me. But now my inner adolescent loves to argue and refuses to believe much of what she says. How do I keep my own need to be right out of the picture?

Bill and I have our own ways of dealing with problems like this, and he tells me, "You're too hard on her. Just ignore what she says. She doesn't really mean it and has lots of issues to deal with." But I know all that. I don't want to hear that what I'm doing is wrong. I'm dealing with lots of issues, too, and I just need for him to see my suffering as well as hers.

When his own mother was dying and we were living in northern Vermont, we invited her to move up from Washington, DC, so that we could help care for her. She refused, and I didn't blame her. She would have been miserable in cold, snowy, rural New England, without friends. Getting her to a hospital where she could undergo kidney dialysis would have meant a two-hour drive across the state several times a week. We didn't want to move and Bill didn't want to leave the job he loved, teaching high school English and running the drama club. So his mother remained at home, with around-the-clock nursing care.

I know Bill felt remorseful when she died alone, without any family members by her side. He seems to have much more patience with my mother than he did with his own. I sometimes think that unconsciously he's trying to make up for what he considers his misdeeds toward his own mom by doting on mine. I try to understand his difficulties, but the ground I walk on is shifting quickly now and I sometimes I feel terribly lost and alone. He always has something kind to say about how Mom is doing or must be feeling. But when it comes to what I'm going through, he mostly tells me how I could make things better by being more patient with her. Letting me know that he sees and hears my frustrations with a big, warm hug would make all the difference in the world to me, but I'm afraid that if I ask him for that, he'll do it because I asked and not because he feels sincere. It's sad that I can't even ask my own husband for help because I fear rejection.

I want a professional opinion about my own behavior, and I decide to contact Dr. Bob, my favorite therapist, whom I haven't seen in some time. Bill and I started seeing him way back, when times were rocky for us as a couple and well before Mom moved here to Virginia. We even took our kids to see him once or twice when communication with them was impossible. But with all of my issues, and in hopes of one day being "fixed," I prefer to see him on my own now. I need as much help as I can get. I worry that one of these days I'm going to lose control altogether and do something I'll regret. Last week was one of the worst I've experienced in a while, and the time feels right to go back to him for more work.

Dr. Bob is gentle and kind, and asks lots of questions without ever forcing his own opinions on me. I've always felt safe telling him my biggest, most shameful secrets. A while back, when I sat in his office sobbing and confused about how I felt about my mother, he smiled and said, "You're doing great! When you can cry like that, you know things are getting better." When I responded, "Are you crazy? Can't you see how much I hurt?" he laughed. I was seriously angry with him, but a few minutes later we laughed together as he showed me another way of looking at my problems.

Right now, Mom is particularly feisty, yelling about little things: "You bought me the wrong brand of dishwashing soap!" or "I need you right now to lift this big, heavy box so I can sort through it!" No matter how careful I am, I'm always saying things that set her off. I know she's in pain both emotionally and physically—she's a shut-in and is reeling from the idea that her life is over—but my emotions are also raw. I find myself panicking and in tears, wondering how in hell I can continue being her caretaker. I want out, feeling imprisoned in a life I hate. There is no one trigger that sets me off. Everything is just upside down and out of control. I sometimes have an overwhelming sense of drowning in my own blood. My moods are without a ray of light, and I spew sarcasm all around me.

I sometimes think about ending it all, imagining how good it would feel to leave it all behind. It's an inviting idea, but when I seriously consider how I might take my life, I come back to the present and change my mind. *If I killed myself, I'd have nothing. Something is better than nothing. Things could change. Things will change!* I feel just a tinge of hope that this stage of my life will pass—soon. In place of allowing my morbid thoughts to rule, I drive by a small, quaint cottage that is for sale on a quiet, tree-lined road in town. I park across the street and fantasize about having a whole house just to myself—no Mom, no Bill. A place where I could start a new life. I'd bring the dogs with me. I'd make art, see friends, and simply be happy.

When I go see Dr. Bob a few days later, he pulls out a small red book and asks me to read several paragraphs out loud. When I'm done, he asks, "Does any of that sound familiar?" I have to admit, "Yes, it sounds just like what I'm going through." He then has me go back a page to read the title of the chapter: "About Post-Traumatic Stress Disorder."

What I read aloud to him described the symptoms and signs that led him to believe that I was struggling with PTSD, including anxiety, depression, panic attacks, thoughts of suicide, and reactions to triggers, like the word "hysterical," which my mother used to describe me whenever I cried as a child. She never employed that term humorously, but in a "she's out of control, annoying, and a pain in the butt" sort of way.

When Dr. Bob suggests that I have PTSD, I lose it. "How can you say that? No! That's impossible! I haven't been through a war, an earthquake, or a terrorist attack. I'm not crazy." I can't even understand what he's talking about—PTSD is a mental illness. I envision my grandmother, locked up in an insane asylum, behaving violently. "I'm *not* like her!"

In response, he offers, "You were beaten as a child, sometimes severely, by your father. You felt abandoned by your mother because she never came to your rescue when you were being beaten. And even the constant act of moving from one house to another, without having a place to call home, was an event that caused trauma."

He goes on and on, citing examples of stories that I've told him, but I still can't accept what he's saying. I end the session abruptly with "No. I am not like that." Dr. Bob responds, "Just think about it."

Once you open up a can of worms the size of Texas, there is no way you can close it up tight again. I start remembering other episodes of abuse. I recognize the passion with which I once denied being beaten when a friend's mother asked me, "Wow, how did you get those black-and-blue marks all over your legs?" She hadn't accused my parents of doing anything, but I knew how those stripes on my legs had gotten there. I lied and told her I had fallen off my bike. I felt very protective of my parents and rushed home to make sure my mother was still there and loved me.

Right now, I don't want to go there. It's too hard. The pain is unbearable. I see Dr. Bob less frequently as the weeks go by. When an appointment is drawing near, I sometimes call him and leave a message. "I can't make it tomorrow. I'll see you next week." The following week, I may call again and leave the same message. I tell myself, *He is way off course with that PTSD thing. I am not crazy! I feel a lot better today, and I'm doing just fine.*

# BREAKING *the* CHAIN

*December 17, 2006*

REMOVING THE TOWEL FROM THE TOP OF THE BOWL, I scoop out the dough that has been rising for the last hour. It's still a bit sticky. I knead in a few more handfuls of flour until it's more elastic and isn't sticking to my fingers. Flattening it out into a rectangle, I roll it in onto itself, like a jelly roll, and tuck it into a bread pan. It will rise a second time before going into the oven.

Baking bread is wonderfully healing when I'm feeling low. With just a few simple ingredients, I can fill the house with irresistible smells. Most loaves allow me to shape them the way I choose to: into a round, an oval, a long, thin baguette, or a dozen or so dinner rolls that I sprinkle with poppy or sesame seeds. I love the squishy feel of the dough in my hands as I punch it down before its final rise. When it's out of the oven and slightly cooled, I slather thick slices with real butter and let it melt into the crumb before I take a bite. It's comfort food at its finest.

These early winter days are dark and drawn out, as if they'll never end. I shed tears easily when I'm alone. I'm extremely tired and not interested in doing much. Reading in front of the fire, or just *being*, are about the only things I feel comfortable doing. My muse has left town. She vows not to return until I start showing up to spend some quality time with her on a regular basis. A portrait of her, as I see her in my mind's eye, hangs above the worktable in my studio, where when I'm at my best I paint, bead, or build collages. She's a colorful lady with an orange body, a large, round burgundy face, and big, happy blue eyes. She has three stars on her forehead, and her hair, in a variety of colors, is spiked and feathery. Around her neck is a choker of flowers, and in the middle of her chest sits a large red heart, inset with outlines of several others. Feathery wings are on either side of the largest heart, so that it can take flight whenever it chooses. She keeps me working, bringing fresh ideas and inspiration when I show up. But I haven't called on her recently. When I take time out, she flies off, wandering through the richness of the world, collecting creative possibilities for another day.

MOM HASN'T HAD A CHEMO treatment in a long time. It was exhausting her, and she began losing weight because she wouldn't eat. She complains that "everything has a metallic taste," and that she isn't hungry anyway. Judging from her low mood, I have a feeling that she's stopped taking the antidepressant the doctor prescribed, and I'm not going to push her to take something she doesn't want to.

She checks in with her oncologist on the phone occasionally, but she rarely shares what he has to say. I'm fairly certain that her doctor stopped the chemo to give her a break, hoping her cancer wouldn't continue to grow. But he is the first to admit that no one knows what is going to happen next.

As Christmas approaches, I'm not in the mood for holiday doings. The kids are traveling on their own this year. Bill and I decide not to prepare the sauerkraut or mushroom and garlic-filled pierogis that we traditionally feast on every year, along with roasted fresh ham and a host of other holiday favorites. Yet I long for a family like the ones I used to find on the cover of the *Saturday Evening Post* many years ago. No one could capture a holiday or the perfect family the way Norman Rockwell did. But this life is no magazine cover, and even the smell of bread in the oven isn't helping my mood to shift out of the ditch today.

The only plan Bill and I have is to go and enjoy a home-cooked meal with good friends who invite us for dinner every Christmas Eve. Mom won't come with us. She likes to be in bed by seven-thirty or eight. Being away for a few hours will give me a chance to get my mind off what is or isn't happening here at home. But that's a few days off. For now I'm trying to be content while I bake bread and catch up on reading several books I've been enjoying.

As I settle into my chair and put my feet up on the hassock, I hear a thud. Mom starts screaming, "Joan, I need you! Joan, come down here!" Usually when she wants something she calls me on the phone.

I rush down to find her on the floor, tangled in the long, thin hose that supplies her with oxygen. She's in pain and struggling to free herself from the web of plastic tubing wrapped around her left leg. I ask, "Where does it hurt?" In tears, she points to her left shoulder. I call 911 and cover her with a blanket to keep her warm. I'm about to burst into tears myself, but my inner dragon suddenly appears, spreading her wings above my shoulders to give me strength. I'm all business—calm, cool, collected. No tears. Mom clutches my hand and says, "I'm scared."

Traffic is heavy as I follow the ambulance to the hospital. I lose sight of it, as holiday shoppers make navigating the roads an effort. Alone in my car, I let a few tears spill out in frustration, but I can't allow them to flow. If I do, I won't be able to hold myself together. Stopped at a red light, I breathe deeply and pray, *Please God, make the light turn green soon so that I can catch up to the ambulance.*

In the emergency room, Mom is placed on a gurney. A nurse checks her vital signs and asks her a number of questions to make sure she is lucid. I sit and wait in the tiny, curtained-off cubicle while she is rushed down to X-ray to have her shoulder checked out. The ER is busy, and in the cubicle next door, someone is moaning in pain.

Back from X-ray, Mom is still very uncomfortable. It's another hour before a doctor comes in and shows us the image of her broken shoulder. Another hour and a half passes before her arm is placed in a sling. She's given painkillers and a prescription for more. She's to report to the doctor's office in two days to be rechecked.

At home I prepare dinner for her and help her get into bed.

She rants, "Why does this have to happen to me? What have I done to deserve this?" The pills are making her unsteady, and I don't sleep well, worrying that if she gets up in the night to use the bathroom, she'll get tangled in the oxygen line again. I'm overwhelmed, believing that this is one more thing that will make her even more dependent on me than she already is.

The next morning, she's up on her own. She sits at her dining table, sorting through pills, trying to figure out what she is supposed to take and when. She whines, "How am I supposed to take care of myself?" When I offer to help her get the pills in order, she tells me, "Just go away. You'll only confuse me."

The painkillers are doing their usual job. Like most narcotics, they usher in her sarcastic and negative behavior. "See? I told you—you're doing it all wrong. Now I'm confused," she complains, as I try my best to help without being too obvious.

The more laid-back and happy I try to be, the angrier she becomes. I prepare some lunch for her, but my resolve begins to dwindle when she smiles and says, "Who said I want a grilled cheese sandwich? Why don't you go outside and leave me alone?" I lose it late in the day and finally tell her, "Shut up and quit complaining." When she continues her tirade, I go off to my room in tears. She knows exactly how to play her cards in order to get me involved in her battles. But no one can say I didn't try.

The next morning, she's barely speaking to me. I know the painkillers have brought this on. She hurts, but what can anyone do except try to keep her pain-free? When we arrive at the doctor's office, I go ahead and hold the door open for her. She snarls, "I don't need you to open doors for me. I'm perfectly all right."

Sitting next to her in the examination room, I tell the doctor, "My mother is an alcoholic. The painkillers are like alcohol for her. She's an addict." Mom is outraged. She responds, "You don't know what you're talking about. You're just an ungrateful kid. I've taken care of you all of your life, and this is what I get?" Pointing at me, she tells the doctor, "My daughter is trying to control my life." At first I don't know if he's getting what's going on here, but he must, because as we leave, he hands me a new prescription for a different painkiller and says softly, "Try this."

Through heavy holiday traffic, Mom continues to rant. She's stuck in her pain and anger, unaware that Christmas is just a few days away. Halfway home, I can't stop the tears that are now flowing freely down my face. She is like a gigantic cat, teasing an injured mouse just before the kill. I decide to take her home before I pick up her new meds. It's very difficult to keep my attention on the road. I'm afraid I'll cause an accident if she doesn't stop this torture.

When we enter the driveway, Mom opens the car door and tries to jump out while the car is still moving. I'm able to stop just before she's completely out the door. Thankfully, she doesn't fall, or we'd have another major problem to deal with. I sit in the car, stunned, as Mom makes her way to the house. Even though I often feel as if Bill isn't supportive of me, I wish he were here at home. I'm sure he could calm her down. I need someone to step in and take over until I can get grounded again.

I feel as if I'm in the middle of an explosive nightmare. I don't know whether to go get Mom's prescription or to stay put until I can think clearly. For the first time ever, I know how it feels to want to hurt someone, and I know I need to get out of here. I feel intense hatred for her and need to talk to someone as soon as possible. I'm scared. I have to catch my breath and regroup before I do something terrible.

After picking up Mom's prescription, I'm calmer. I phone Bill to ask him to come home immediately, and then I call a meditation teacher in the insight meditation community. She's a psychologist, and I know her to be very kind and compassionate. She can see me in an hour, but for only twenty minutes. When she detects my distress, she suggests that I immediately go to the hospital where Mom has been treated for her cancer. She tells me to ask to speak with the chaplain, whom she knows and respects and who she is sure will help me.

At the hospital, I sit alone in the chaplain's waiting room, weeping and worried she won't have time to see me. I'm sure she has more important things to deal with than my little problems. I think maybe I should just go home.

A few minutes later, a calm and elegant, gray-haired woman comes down the hall and invites me into her office. I begin to tell her my story. She listens without stopping me. Her face is kind. I can see concern in her eyes. I feel as though caring arms are holding me. As she explains that she regularly deals with problems that caretakers of the elderly run into, my breathing slows down and gets deeper. When I suddenly panic because it's dinnertime and I need to go home and feed Mom, she assures me that it's okay. She tells me I need to take care of myself first, right now. She's given me permission to take care of me—something I haven't done in a long time. She is helping to reassure me that the way I feel is important, too. That it's okay to take time out when I'm feeling low and that it's okay to ask for what I need.

She suggests that I get Mom into respite care at a local nursing home for a week or so. Doing that would give both of us a chance to be away from each other and would give me time to think about what needs to happen next. She also gives me the telephone number of a psychologist she says would be a great help, and the name and phone number of a woman who has been through a similar situation. She assures me that I'm not alone and that things will be okay once I learn how to manage these problems by taking more time to care for myself.

Back at home, Mom and I speak to each other, but our words are tense and awkward. I know she is hurting and feels as enslaved by this life as I do. Without telling her what we're up to, Bill and I make an appointment the next morning at the nursing home. Before we can move forward, we need to see what the place is like and ask if they can take her for a week. On our inspection, it appears to be a well-run facility, very clean and new to the community. The rooms are comfortable, and, yes, Mom could bring her cat along if she wishes. When I tell them what they'll be up against, they assure me that they deal with those kinds of problems every day. We make arrangements to deliver Mom in two days.

Worried that she won't go along with the plan, I imagine the coming battle, in which she will claim, "You're throwing me out. Just like my mother did. And at Christmas, no less."

Bill broaches the subject with her so that she can't hold me responsible. Over a bowl of coffee ice cream, he kindly suggests that we all need a vacation from each other. "You know how it gets during the holidays. We're all tired, and you've had a tough week. You'll be well taken care of and pampered if you agree to go into respite care at a gorgeous facility Joan and I visited this morning. It'll be for only a week, and you'll get a chance to relax."

Surprisingly, she is open and happy to be getting away. She's even a bit excited as she hurriedly begins packing a small bag to take with her.

# THE SECOND TIME AROUND

*December 20, 2006*

MOM IS READY TO GO ON WHAT SHE IS NOW CALLING her "getaway." She's packed a few mystery novels, dark chocolate, and cigarettes. Smoking inside the nursing home is forbidden. I'm not sure that she understands that, but I'm not bringing it up. While she is away, nurses will dispense her meds when she is supposed to take them. All of her needs will be met. I just hope that she finds some pleasure in being away, rather than being surrounded by the same old four walls here at home.

Her mood is a bit better today, but I'm still trying to stay out of her way. Her shoulder is painful. She can't find a comfortable way to hold her arm in the sling and is constantly rearranging it and getting it messed up every time she tries to make it better.

Tomorrow morning we'll take her to the nursing home and

get her settled in. Though I desperately need the break, it feels strange and awkward that we won't be seeing her on Christmas. I suddenly can't decide whether this is really the right thing to do. I was so relieved when the chaplain said I'd have a week to myself without Mom in the house, but now my old control issues are kicking in.

I'm still in shock from the events of the past few days. Part of me wants my life back and needs a break from being with my mother. But the take-control, responsible, good-daughter part of me is stuck in place, wanting to make sure that Mom will get everything she needs. My thoughts are confused. Am I addicted to this misery? Will I want to go and see her every day to make sure that she's all right? Will one week be long enough? Will she want to stay there? Or will she insist upon coming home before the week is up? I'm in a bottomless pit of my own making, trying to climb out and find what's best for all of us.

Instead of allowing myself to continue my crazy thinking, I think of the Buddha, put a smile on my face, and with one foot in front of the other, march forward, envisioning the week filled with peace and time to relax. I gather stamps, pens, and other paraphernalia to begin writing personal notes on our annual Christmas letter.

Suddenly I hear Mom screaming. "Oh my God, now what?" I ask, racing down the stairs to see what's happening. Again she is lying on the floor, tangled in the oxygen line and shrieking in pain. "I think my leg is broken," she says. I know the drill. I call 911, alert Bill to what is happening, and cover her with a blanket. Once again, I find myself in emergency mode. I'm numb and just keep doing what has to done.

When the ambulance arrives, the EMTs gingerly load her

onto a gurney and lift her inside the back of the van. She begs me to go along with her. She says she wants to hold my hand. Mom begs the driver to turn off the siren. She cries, "It embarrasses me." Bill follows in the car.

I'm sitting in the front seat next to the driver. Two EMTs check Mom's vital signs. There is no room for me back there, but the door between the compartments is open. Mom keeps calling, "Are you there, Joan?" and I keep responding, "Yes, Mom, I'm here. Everything is going to be all right." She needs to hear me and know that I haven't abandoned her. I feel better up front in the cab, knowing that I'm off the hook and somebody else is in charge of her. My neck lengthens out from between my shoulders, where I stuff it when I'm anxious and upset. I'm like a turtle during times like this, pulling back into my shell, trying to protect myself from what is happening around me. My dragon must be taking a nap, tired from the broken-shoulder incident.

Bill arrives at the hospital right behind the ambulance. We sit in the waiting room, not speaking but holding hands, until they have moved Mom into a cubicle in the ER. I'm shivering, though it isn't cold.

Half an hour later, we go in. Nurses are getting Mom ready to once again go to X-ray. She's hooked up to all sorts of machines monitoring her heart and breathing. She's drowsy, and I presume the IV is dosing her with pain relief.

Again, the ER is bustling. Doctors and nurses come and go. They check up on somebody next door who apparently has food poisoning. Down the hall, they are monitoring a woman who just had a heart attack. There is nothing private in the ER. You can hear it all and feel better or worse, depending on whether the patient next door is going to live or die. If you're a private person, like I am, it's not a comforting place to be. Bill and I head to the waiting room, where there is less tension in the air. Thirty minutes later, when we return, Mom is back from X-ray.

The same doctor who took care of her just a few days ago is there with her. He tells us that she has a spiral fracture of the femur. "She'll probably be spending at least a week in the hospital. She needs surgery to repair the broken bone and needs to be stable before she goes home." The leg fracture and the broken shoulder are both on the left side of her body, and obviously she won't be moving around much on her own for a long time. My head is filled with unanswerable questions, like *How will I be able to take care of her?*

WE'VE BEEN AT THE HOSPITAL for four hours. It's almost dinnertime, and I'm hungry. The cafeteria doesn't have anything that looks appetizing. We follow as Mom is moved upstairs to the room that will be hers for the next week.

She will have surgery tomorrow morning; a rod will be placed in her leg and the bone pinned back together. Her roommate is asleep. I kiss Mom good-bye and tell her I'll be back the next day. She doesn't hear me.

Down in the parking lot, it's dark. A few snowflakes fall and melt as they land on my coat sleeve. Around the hospital grounds, homes are aglow with Christmas lights, Green and red, some blinking or some not. A life-size plastic snowman and a plastic Rudolph, with his bulbous red nose, celebrate the winter darkness.

## THE GHOSTS *of* CHRISTMAS PAST

*December 25, 2006*

DECEMBER ALWAYS SETS OFF A FLOOD OF MEMORIES of Christmases gone by. This one will top the list of the worst and will only add to my discomfort at this time of year. As a kid, I loved Christmas. The tree, the wreath, the carols, and the gifts had my undivided attention. And even though I loved the Baby Jesus story, Santa was my man. I tried staying awake all night on Christmas Eve so that I could catch a glimpse of him. But like every other kid I knew, I fell fast asleep and never heard the *kaboom* I thought might wake me when Rudolph and the gang arrived on my roof.

When I found out that Santa wasn't real, I rummaged around the house when my mother was out, looking for the stash of gifts she hid. A big part of my excitement was about outsmarting her; the other part was about finding out what I would be receiving—hopefully all of the things I wanted most, like the *Alice in Wonderland* doll I asked for one year. She wore a blue dress and had long, straight blond hair that I loved to comb. I tried curling her hair with rollers the instant she was mine, but it didn't work. I loved her anyway and was very much assured that Mom loved me, too. Otherwise, she wouldn't have given Alice to me.

When Bill and I got married, we happily went about making the holidays our own. When Mark and Lisa arrived on the scene, Christmas got even better. As tots, they loved playing with the gift wrap, ribbons, and boxes more than with what was inside them. I loved watching as they tried to stay awake every Christmas Eve, waiting for Santa to arrive, just like I had. But there were always way too many gifts under the tree, and the holiday became about expectation and "I want," rather than about the concept of giving. As our kids got older, Bill and I came to our senses and put fewer presents under the tree. We often chose a local family, identified by tags hanging from the Christmas tree at one of the local shops, to provide with Christmas dinner and gifts for their children. Our own celebration became more about the delicious food we prepared than about "getting" things and keeping up with the Joneses.

In 1987, I gave up on Christmas altogether. My mother was still living in New Hampshire. We invited her and my brothers to get away from the land of ice and snow to visit with our family in Virginia for the holidays. I thought my invitation would be a wonderful way to bring us together with those members of the family we rarely got to see.

I envisioned a real Christmas celebration. Though there likely would be no snow or icicles hanging from the eaves, I imagined the aromas of our traditional holiday meal, logs burning in the fireplace, Handel's Messiah playing in the background. The tree would be small but beautiful. There would be a holly wreath on the door, and the guest room, ready for Mom, would be decked out with red and green Christmas pillows on her bed. My brothers agreed to sleep on cots in my office/studio space. I happily buzzed around, baking Christmas goodies before their arrival and believed I had neared perfection in my planning.

They arrived two days before Christmas, packed in Mom's car, as the sun was about to set. Though the weather was more typical of late October than December, I had a fire crackling on the hearth and had prepared a pot of everyone's favorite chicken soup. I topped it off with a salad and bread that I had baked myself.

The first sign of trouble was my needing to remind my brother Reid that we were a smoke-free home and he'd have to go outside to smoke his hand-rolled cigarettes. Still, I thought all would be well.

On Christmas Eve morning, Reid came to breakfast in a black mood. "I need another place to sleep. I cannot stay in the same room with Zed." He was upset by something that had happened between the two of them. Both in their thirties, they apparently still had lots of issues. Not wanting to get involved in their troubles, we agreed to set up Reid's cot in Bill's office. That afternoon, we took a hike on a nearby nature trail and spent the rest of the day just being together. Everyone seemed happy and content.

Christmas morning found us sitting around the tree, sipping cups of steaming coffee and freshly squeezed orange juice, and eating blueberry boy bait, our traditional holiday breakfast cake. The fresh ham, for our late-afternoon dinner, was already in the oven. We took turns opening gifts, examining the sometimes hilarious contents of the stockings we'd prepared for everyone. There were formal bow ties for my hippie brothers, along with Superman comic books and racy ballpoint pens that, when held in a certain way, showed a female figure in the barrel, stripped of her hula skirt and bra.

As we started gathering up torn wrapping paper and the crumbs from breakfast, Mom decided to hand out her gifts. They were always checks placed formally in envelopes with "Merry Christmas from Mother" written across the front. She'd given up buying gifts long ago, preferring to give checks so that the recipients could use the money toward something they needed. She'd recently been upping the ante for Mark and Lisa, who were now practically adults. Mark was already in college, and Lisa was in her junior year of high school. That year was no exception. She gave them each two hundred bucks.

When Reid saw how much money she had given them, he exploded with the force of a tornado, yelling, "Mom, that's not fair. You gave me half of that. Why do you do that? What are you trying to prove?" He asked her how much she had given to his ten-year-old-son, Jesse, who was in New Hampshire, celebrating the holiday with his mother and her new husband. "Is it the same amount as you gave Mark and Lisa?" He'd obviously forgotten that Mom often paid his taxes, along with his dental bills. At the end of his tirade, he threw his own check into the fire, letting it burn. Zed followed suit.

Mark and Lisa quickly made their way to their rooms while Bill and I sat speechless, unable to figure out what had just happened. Mom was raging at my brothers, setting the tone for the rest of their visit. "You boys are never grateful for what I do for you. Take me to the airport now! I need to get out of here. I don't want to be with you!"

But there were no flights leaving Charlottesville for points north on Christmas day, so she was forced to wait until the next morning. She poured her anger into my own personal space just because she was mad as hell at my brothers. She went on and on about them. I kept quiet, trying not to get involved. Bill put on his "good-guy hat" and tried making everything better, saying, "They'll come to their senses." But this time their boo-boo was way too big.

We ate dinner in hostile silence. None of us was particularly hungry. My gut felt filled to the brim with shrapnel, and I was carrying bushels of radioactive matter inside my head that might leak out if I didn't pay close attention to keeping it contained. I was angry with my brothers, and I didn't appreciate Mom's trying to get me involved in the battle.

Our usual Christmas evening plans included going to a showing of one of the new blockbuster films that opened on Christmas Day. On that particular night, it seemed important to get out of the house and somehow break the spell that had swallowed all of us up in one swift gulp. But what to see?

Mom retired to her room, and the rest of us couldn't decide what to do. At the last minute, my brothers chose to see a show at a nearby theater. Tired from the events of the day, and without thinking, Bill and I went along with them. It wasn't until we got to the theater that we realized we were about to see *Throw Momma from the Train*, starring Danny DeVito and Billy Crystal.

I was horror-stricken. Why had my brothers chosen that film, about a man who tries to get his creative-writing teacher to kill his abusive mother? Was it a coincidence, or were they trying to be funny? I didn't ask them, knowing I'd get an answer I didn't want to hear. It was a highly difficult situation for two movie buffs like Bill and me. We always read reviews and synopses of the latest that Hollywood has to offer before spending money to see them. Why hadn't we picked up on the title before we left home? My shame and embarrassment about that night are still so thick and heavy that I've never been able to shovel my way through it.

More bickering and fighting happened around the breakfast table the next morning. Growing more assertive than before, Mom announced in front of my brothers, "I want you, Joan, to be the executor of my estate. I don't want your brothers involved with anything that has to do with my finances—ever." She couldn't have been more unpleasant if she had been wearing a witch's hat. Zed and Reid thought she'd leave them nothing. They left the table, their faces mirroring our mother's rage. My answer to Mom was "No, I won't do that. I don't want to be caught up in the middle of this war." As angry with me now as she was with my brothers, she left for the airport in a huff. By late afternoon, she was back in New Hampshire. The next day, my brothers left Virginia, dropping Mom's car off at her house without comment.

I never imagined I'd get entangled in such family insanity, nor did I believe I'd be recounting it here, to people I may have never met before. Though to some it may sound like a comedy sketch, none of it was or is funny to me. I can still feel the anger and hatred that my family members spewed at each other during those few days. We each had unpredictable roles in the script, which included my own search for Christmas perfection and my unsuccessful attempt to be a neutral element in the battle of the century.

After my brothers left, I gave in to sheer exhaustion. In big capital letters, I put us on the top of the list of the world's most dysfunctional families. The worst part of it was that we all went about our own lives, forgetting how hurtful we had been to each other. Though Bill and I speak about that Christmas occasionally, no one ever mentioned it again when we got together as a "family." I was left with the belief that Christmas with my family of origin would always be a time of insanity, and my lack of enthusiasm for the holidays hasn't changed since then.

# WHAT'S NEXT?

*December 26, 2006*

THE HOUSE IS EERILY QUIET BUT FOR CLEO'S MEOWING for Mom. They had a regular evening game in which Cleo would get up on Mom's bed and slither under the blanket. Mom tickled the top of it as Cleo tried to catch the invisible hand that made the blanket move. When Mom climbed into bed and turned off the light, Cleo snuggled up against her side. The poor cat is lonely without her. Every day I invite her upstairs, but she's afraid of Bill and the dogs. I don't know what we're going to do with her. We have two cats of our own, who aren't particularly tolerant of her. When they see each other outside, they give each other plenty of space but hiss and growl.

Though Mom's difficulties are out of control and happening quickly, it's a relief to have just Bill and the animals for company. Mom is still in the hospital but will be discharged the day after tomorrow. Her doctor wants her to spend some healing time in bed before beginning to learn to walk again. It would be impossible for me to care for her here at home and transport her to a rehab facility on a daily basis.

I try to digest that along with what her oncologist suggested when he visited her after her leg surgery. He encouraged me to get hospice involved with her care immediately. "There is nothing more I can do for your mother. Her death is not imminent, but it's not that far off. It could be six weeks or six months. Most families make the mistake of waiting until the last few days of a loved one's life before they call hospice." He noted that they'd be a huge help to me, as well as to Mom.

I am bewildered by the concept of Mom's learning to walk again and getting hospice involved at the same time. It seems counterintuitive. Calling in hospice seems to be giving up, while having her learn to walk again is anything but. Her quality of life is of the utmost importance in my eyes. Perhaps being able to walk, even if it's with a walker or a cane, will bring her some peace and pleasure. On the other hand, I've been told that once an ailing elder falls and has serious injuries, it's over. They give up on themselves and simply waste away. These days, a doctor's role in eldercare seems to be about keeping patients alive as long as possible, no matter their quality of life. Will the nursing home she'll be living in be a positive influence when it comes to her happiness? She's been dead set against nursing homes all along, but now she has no choice.

I have so many questions. We need to find a nursing home with a rehabilitation facility for Mom in two days. That's today and tomorrow. When we walk through the doors of the first one we visit, the smell of urine greets us. There is no one at the reception desk. When the receptionist finally returns, she tells us that they do have a bed available and asks a nurse to give us a tour of the facility.

The dining room where residents have their meals looks like an old gymnasium with a stage at one end. I envision basketball hoops on either side of the room. Our footsteps echo through the room as we walk across the hardwood floor. The bedrooms look out onto an inner courtyard planted with flowers, shrubs, and trees. Televisions are blaring from several rooms. A white-haired man sits in a wheelchair, staring at his feet. I say, "Hello, how are you today?" He doesn't respond. A younger woman without clothes on runs down the hall, giggling, while a nurse follows, trying to round her up. "Come back here, Mrs. Robins; you need to get dressed," she pleads. Signs of death and decay are evident everywhere. Besides the obvious decline in the health of the residents, the grass needs mowing outside, the walls need paint, and the elevator to the top floor, which houses the rehabilitation center, is very old and very small. Can a wheelchair really fit inside it?

In the rehab center, the occupational therapist greets us and explains, "Your mom's work will begin immediately as we try to keep her body parts moving and strong while she is healing. She'll eventually use a walker to get around, and just maybe she'll be able to walk again on her own." Given that I've just been told my mother won't be with us much longer, my mind refuses to accept the concept that Mom could be walking on her own again. I leave feeling morose and more confused than ever. Where is the map I need that will tell me where to go and what to do?

Back at the hospital, I talk to Mom's social worker, who wants to help us get her settled somewhere. But she can't tell us what to do; she can only make suggestions and give us a list of what we need to be thinking about. I wish there were somebody who could take over and steer me in the right direction. Bill is at an appointment that he scheduled weeks ago. I wish he were here to help me ask the right questions and to explain the things I can't get straight in my head.

Though I may look calm, I'm in panic mode. My gut is tangled in pulsing knots. I need to stay close to a bathroom to keep from crapping all over myself. I'm the only one who hears the unanswerable *God, what am I going to do?* that echoes through my mind. The sudden events of the last week have left me feeling like a fine porcelain teacup flying through the air, about to shatter into a million pieces.

When Bill returns to the hospital, he tells me that he stopped to see another nursing home with a rehab center and, yes, they will have a bed when Mom is discharged. He says that they are waiting for a resident, now finished with rehab, to leave. The space could be available by tomorrow night. It's a fairly new, one-story facility. It doesn't smell, and the administrator he talked to was very nice.

When Bill takes me there to see for myself, I find it's the exact opposite of the first home we visited. The building is new and attractive. Dinner is being served when we arrive. The residents are eating what looks like delicious, healthy food in a real dining room setting; the tables are set with white tablecloths and white cloth napkins. No one is running around naked. We'll know tomorrow morning when the bed will be available.

I don't know what I would do without Bill. He holds me, lets me cry, and assures me that once Mom is settled in her new space, I'll have time to recover my own being and it'll be just us. We haven't had quality time alone together since our last trip to the beach. We haven't even eaten a meal together in over a week. Our bed goes unmade. We rush back and forth to walk and feed the dogs and cats. We have few moments to relax and allow the burdens of each day to fall away. I need to find my center and feel solid ground beneath me. Bill and I need to reconnect and dust away the cobwebs of neglect that fill our lives. Once Mom is established in a nursing home, we plan to catch up on sleep, go to see a bunch of funny movies, cook delicious meals, and maybe even get away for a few days.

Mom isn't happy about her situation. She knows I can't take care of her at home. She's doing the best she can. The doctors have her on high doses of pain meds. Some times she is more coherent than others. Occasionally she doesn't know where she is. On Christmas Eve, close to midnight, she calls us from the hospital and begs, "Please come get me. I'm being held prisoner; they're being mean to me. Come get me. I want to leave." When I mention her call to her the next morning, she doesn't know what I'm talking about. When I ask her if she understands that she will be moved to a nursing home, she says she does.

Thankfully, she is being very sweet and nice to the nurses and doctors who are working with her at the hospital, but I worry how she'll react when she's moved to the nursing home tomorrow afternoon. She can be a hermit, preferring her own company. But I think being with people other than Bill and me will be good for her. She tends to forget her own troubles when she hears other people's stories. And she adores gossip.

# MOVING DAY

*December 29, 2006*

MOM WAS MOVED TO THE NURSING HOME TODAY in the late afternoon by ambulance. I wasn't there when she arrived. I plan on going to see her after dinner tonight, but just before I sit down to eat, the phone rings. In tears, she says, "I'm in terrible pain. The nurses won't medicate me. It hurts bad. Do something."

Ten minutes later, I find Mom in a room by herself, looking extremely uncomfortable. She's lying lopsided on her bed. Her left side, where the bones are broken, is elevated on pillows. She looks as though she's going to roll out of the bed if she moves just the slightest bit.

I ask a nurse, "Why won't you give her pain meds? She's suffering severely." She leaves the room without answering me. I hear scurrying out in the hall, and another nurse arrives, asking if she can help me. I tell her, "My mother is in terrible pain and needs to take something so that she can get some sleep and begin the healing process."

She answers, "Well, the hospital didn't send any meds with her." When I ask if they have called the hospital to find out why, she replies, "No."

I respond, "Please call the hospital and find out when they can get her medication here. In the meantime, give her something to ease her pain."

"I can call the hospital, but I cannot give your mother anything for her pain unless a doctor directs it."

I know there is a doctor connected with this nursing home. "Why don't you call the facility doctor and ask for permission to give her a painkiller?"

"I can't do that. The doctor is at home now."

The ever-protective dragon who resides within me is always at the ready to help me navigate difficult situations. She comes out roaring, flapping her wings and spitting fire. I hear myself saying, "I don't care where the doctor is. Just get the doctor on the phone and ask for some pain meds for a woman who is in severe pain."

She quickly leaves the room. The next thing I know, I'm arguing with the doctor on the phone. I don't give her a chance to make any excuses; I simply tell her my demands.

When she says, "The meds will arrive tomorrow morning." I tell her, "That isn't good enough. Come down here now and give my mother the medication she needs."

A few minutes later, I'm talking to the administrator of the home on the phone. I seem to be making an impression. Glad for the recognition, my dragon heats up even more. She loves being in control.

When I tell the woman that Mom looks as though she could easily roll out of bed, and ask for rails to hold her in, she tells me it's against the law to use rails on the beds. I tell her, "I don't care what the law says. If my mother falls out of bed, I will file a lawsuit against the home. I'm not going anywhere until my mother is given some medication for her pain and there are rails on her bed." I hang up the phone without listening for a response.

Everyone has disappeared. I assume they're regrouping. The owner of the home has been called. I explain to him what is happening, ending with, "I will not leave until my mother is being cared for properly."

The nursing home doctor arrives next. She wants to explain why she isn't supposed to give my mother medication until she gets clearance from the hospital. I tell her, "Give my mother some medication, or the nursing home's name will make headlines in the morning."

In the meantime, Mom's painful moaning gets louder. A new bed is wheeled in with rails. Two aides slide it in place next to Mom's bed and lift her on the sheet she is lying on. I watch in horror as they drop her onto the new bed with a thud. Mom cries out. The aides quickly disappear down the hall, as the nurses come back in with the doctor, who gives Mom a shot for her pain. They elevate her left side again with pillows. Everything that I asked for has been done. However, their bedside manner leaves much to be desired. My gut is roiling, and I'm feeling as though I could punch someone. When I try to speak, all that comes out is a stutter.

Who told me, "Once Mom is in good hands, everything will be fine"? Are these the good hands we'll be depending on for God knows how long? When I visited this nursing home several days ago, I was so relieved to find a place where I thought my mother would be safe and well taken care of. The unforgivable events of this evening tell me otherwise. I've heard horror stories about nursing homes, but I thought this one might be different. We're out of options. The only other facility with rehab doesn't have a great reputation, and moving her again would be a nightmare. From what I've heard, this place has the best rehabilitation unit of all. I suppose I need to give it time. I'm on the cold, windy plains of eldercare on my own. I have no idea of what to do next, and I imagine that what I am doing is all wrong.

I hate confrontation and fear; I prefer peaceful exchanges to the battle I brought on this evening. My dragon is often a source of embarrassment to me. She appears when terrible things arise and arrives so quickly that I rarely, if ever, have time to pause before I become a raving lunatic. But even with her here to help me, I find it difficult to let her rant. I can't say how many times I've walked away from a battle feeling like a loser, even though I was in the right and had won the war. Though I'm terribly embarrassed by my behavior, I also feel good about standing up for Mom. I'm responsible for her. She was being treated poorly. My job is to make things better for her. I suppose I sometimes have to play my highest cards, even if doing so brings me pain.

I sit beside Mom's bed until she falls asleep, then trudge out the door for home. As I pass the nurses' station, all conversation stops. I tell them with great satisfaction, "Good night. I'll see you in the morning."

The night is cold. There are no stars. My dragon folds her wings, puts out her fire, and retires for the night. Now I can cry.

# SETTLING IN

*December 30, 2006*

WHEN I CHECK IN AT THE NURSING HOME THE NEXT morning, I find Mom has a roommate—Roseanne—and when I pause at their door and listen for a moment, I hear them comparing notes. Mom isn't in pain, and whatever they're giving her doesn't seem to be making her aggressive or nasty. Roseanne had a light stroke several months ago and is almost ready to be discharged. She sounds very cheerful and optimistic about being at home with her sister, who is five years younger than she is. I can't help but think that being in a place like this, with other people to talk to, is good for Mom. Though she can be reclusive, she's been stuck with just Bill and me for months now. No wonder we don't get along. She needs other folks to share thoughts with who are more in tune with her stage of life. Bill and I don't know what this aging thing is really all about yet, so we're not the most empathic people to be around. And though Mom won't be able to get out of bed for a while, once she starts rehab she'll begin using a wheelchair and will be able to go to the dining room and begin conversing with more folks and making new friends.

I'm relieved to see things going smoothly, at least for the moment. The new crew of nurses and aides on duty are all very nice and seem to be giving Mom a good deal of attention; they appear to be unaware that I caused some "trouble" last night. But I'm still worried about what will happen next. While I don't think last night's scenario bodes well, I need to see how it unfolds as time passes. Giving her care over to people I don't know is a whole new experience for me, and Mom's never been in a nursing home before, so it's new for her, too.

I'm caught between needing to relax and take some personal time for myself, and needing to be on guard and alert. Though I'm relieved to have her gone, I'm easily stressed by the smallest glitches, and now that Mom's been living downstairs for six years, I'm used to our everyday grind and the dysfunctional games we've played. Without her directing me from the background, I hope I'll become more grounded and can get back to my own artistic life.

I'm reminded of when Lisa, my youngest child, went off to school for the first time. I walked across the street to the bus stop with her, and when she climbed onboard and was driven out of sight, I cried. I was excited about the idea that I'd have from eight in the morning till three in the afternoon to myself, but it took me weeks to actually start the projects I had planned to begin when both kids were finally in school full-time. I didn't know what to do with all that free time at first. When I finally got into my own groove, I had difficulty changing "hats" when the kids arrived home in the afternoon and I had to stop my creative work and start being a mom again.

When they left as adults to begin their own lives, a similar thing happened: it took some time for me to fill my empty nest with exciting projects and the reality that I was my own being. Of course I missed them, but when they came home for a vacation, I was always happy to see them go their own ways when it was over. Such is the life of a mother. And here I am, being a mother to my own mother. Will this separation be any different?

On New Year's Day, Mom calls in the morning to say she has the flu, as do her roommate and most of the other "guests" in the facility. When I check in on her at noon, she is sitting in the same puddle of diarrhea she was sitting in when she called me. Should I raise another ruckus at the nurses' station? I'm doubtful that the staff will do their jobs properly, but a nurse apologizes to both Mom and me, explaining that "half of the staff didn't show up for work today, either because it's a holiday and they were out partying all night or because they're also sick themselves." She promises to have Mom cleaned up within half an hour. The nursing home is getting big bucks for its services, and Mom is here so that someone else can tend to her. Rather than causing another scene, I decide to go home and call her in an hour or two to see how she is.

At home, I lie down and sleep for an hour. I wake overwhelmed by the pile of laundry that sits next to the washing machine. My houseplants are wilting and need to be watered. I have to walk the dogs, and if I don't go out to the grocery store, we'll be going out to eat again. We've been to all the decent restaurants in town over the past few weeks, and all I want now is my own good, home-cooked food. Besides, our wallets are close to empty, just like the fridge, where the carrots in the veggie drawer look like they've been around the world and back. They're soft to the touch and wrinkly. The lettuce is all brown around the edges and beginning to rot.

At the grocery store, I run into my friend Carol. I haven't seen her in a while, and she tells me she's been worried about me. "You look exhausted. You're in way over your head," she remarks, as she presses a piece of paper into my hand. On it is written the phone number of a nurse friend of hers who has been in a similar situation. Carol has already told Amy about me, and Amy is expecting me to call her. Although the idea of contacting someone I don't know for help continues to go against everything I've been taught, my recent talks with Dr. Bob have underscored that I have to reach out, despite my difficulty, so I can recover from this crazy period in my life.

Back at home, with Bill pitching in, I prepare a frittata with fresh mushrooms, sweet red peppers, onions, garlic, cheddar cheese, and spinach in the mix. A salad of crisp romaine, avocado, orange slices, and toasted pecans completes the meal. I love simple food, and this repast fills the empty feeling my body has been telling me I need to do something about.

THE NEXT MORNING, I STUFF my fear into my back pocket and call Amy to introduce myself. She's been through difficult times with her own mother. As a nurse, she has seen how caretakers are often broken by the work involved in caring for their aging parents. I feel close to her as I babble on about my own troubles. Tears leak out onto the table in front of me. She kindly says, "Take your time. It's okay. I can talk as long as you need to." Nobody I have spoken to lately has taken time to hear me and recognize my pain. I'm grateful and love this person whom I have never met and cannot see. There is only her voice coming to me from some unknown place.

We talk for over an hour. She says, "Your only concern right now must be *you*. The nursing home will or won't screw up, and there's nothing you can do about it. Call hospice and get them involved. They will take care of everything. If you don't get some rest and time away from your mother, you're going to make yourself sick."

The next morning, I get on the phone and talk with a helpful person about hospice. I imagine it will take a while for them to get everything together, but to my surprise, by midafternoon a nurse and a social worker have a plan to meet with us at the facility two days from now. The next step is to get Mom on board with it.

Dreading that conversation, I put off talking to her about it until the evening before the meeting. But when Bill and I go to visit and prep her for this new scheme, she's already asleep. She looks better than she has in days. Her face has some color, and she looks comfortable with a yellow blanket pulled up to her chin. We decide to return in the morning to talk with her.

As we leave, the head nurse, with whom I dealt with on that first stormy night, stops us in the hallway. She addresses me alone, as if Bill is invisible. In a snippy tone, she tells me, "Dr. E. has put your mother on Vicodin because she's in so much pain." I groan and say, "That is one of the narcotics that brings out Mom's anger and makes her hard to deal with." She also tells me that the facility's social worker visited with Mom earlier that afternoon and went over her "do not resuscitate" order. Mom signed it when she was in the hospital after she broke her leg. The nurse smiles and says, "Your mom tore it up on the spot. She told us, 'I don't need that anymore. I want to go back on chemo.'"

When I tell her that, according to Mom's oncologist, chemo is not an option and that hospice will be overseeing her care beginning tomorrow afternoon, she becomes angry. "Your mother is not dying. You are giving up on her. She will not like this!" Bill asks her not to mention hospice to Mom before we have a chance to tell her about it ourselves. The nurse stomps off down the hall, shaking her head.

We're both stunned. Who does she think she is? As I watch her walk away, my stomach begins to twist with anxiety. Here is another painful reminder that my new role comes with significant growing pains and a steep learning curve.

## MEETING *the* MINDS

*January 10, 2007*

AT NINE SHARP THE NEXT MORNING, THE PHONE rings. It's Anna, the social worker at the nursing home. "I have some real concerns about your mother and her care. I'd like to meet with you and the rest of the staff, along with your mother."

I ask, "What's the problem?"

She replies, "Let's talk about it later."

It sounds and feels ominous. Does the nursing home have it in for me because I made a scene that first night? I'm jittery and snap at Bill when he says, "You're making too big a deal out of this. They just want to make sure everyone is on the same page."

Meanwhile, I rush to meet with a Ms. Allen, who heads up the Alzheimer's Association and with whom I have a ten o'clock appointment to chat about Mom. Before she was hospitalized, we noticed Mom was extremely forgetful and confused at times. A friend encouraged me to get more information about Alzheimer's and dementia in general.

I tell Ms. Allen what has been transpiring and say I'm anxious about the meeting with the staff at the facility. "I'm worried they're going to drop a bomb of some kind."

Ms. Allen assures me, "What you did the other night is what you had to do. You are in the right. The nursing home didn't treat your mother well."

Right or wrong, I envision the honchos at the facility blaming me for causing a major disruption the other night. Old patterns of fear often keep me from standing up for myself. Under circumstances like that, I fill up with shame and terror, which make me want to melt into the floor.

In discussing Mom's forgetfulness and confusion, Ms. Allen says, "It doesn't sound like your mom has Alzheimer's. It does sound like she has some dementia setting in, though I doubt it's advanced. It's going to happen, and, for your own sake, she needs to be in a nursing home. Take care of yourself. Don't worry too much about her. She'll be taken care of."

I feel slightly relieved, but my patterns of worry, imagining the worst, and taking the blame for most things began years ago in my childhood. Even when I know I'm right, I feel guilty until I'm proven innocent. Just passing a police car parked on the side of the road used to cause me to panic that I had done something wrong. I obviously have an issue with authority figures. I've always believed everybody else knows much more than I do, and often I feel the need to prove myself so that I don't feel incompetent. That's usually when my dragon shows up.

Knowing that things are heating up, Bill goes to see Mom on his own, to fill her in on the hospice meeting. When he arrives at her bedside, he discovers the nurses have already told her about it. She is extremely angry and asks, "Where the hell is Joan?" Bill, being the honest soul that he is, tells her that I am meeting with a woman from the Alzheimer's Association. Mom explodes. "I do not have Alzheimer's. Joan is an interfering bitch. She needs to get out of my life." Mom would never consider that Bill, the "good guy," could be part of this terrible conspiracy that I, the "bad guy," have cooked up against her. That drug Vicodin is in command. Otherwise she wouldn't be in attack mode.

When I arrive in Mom's room thirty minutes before the meeting, she starts ranting, "I don't have Alzheimer's. You're obviously telling everyone that I do." She calls me a stupid witch and says, "You called hospice. You're trying to take control of my life. Who the hell do you think you are?"

There is nothing I can say that will calm her down. The more I try, the louder and angrier she gets.

The staff begins to arrive. There is Anna, the social worker, the facility doctor, the head nurse, and the administrator. Anna begins the meeting, asking me, "What are your concerns for your mother?" Shaking inside, I explain that Mom's comfort and well-being are my chief worries. Doing my best to keep my dragon in check, I calmly apologize for having been so difficult on Mom's first night at the home. "I am the one responsible for my mother's care. She called me to ask for my help. Mom told me that she needed medication for her pain and that you folks wouldn't help her. I will never ignore her needs. I responded in the way any family member would have, and when you refused to take proper care of her, I had to intervene. I am sure that if the circumstances had been reversed and you had been in my shoes, all of you would have done the same thing. At least I hope so."

I continue, being brutally honest and clear about Mom's alcoholism, her emotional reactions to certain drugs, and her attacks on me. "Life in our household has not been easy, and we have all done the best we can. I want my mother to be happy and comfortable wherever she is. I can no longer take care of her myself. My greatest concern for her is that you will look after her needs and care for her as you might for your own mothers."

While I speak, Mom sits in her bed, pouting like a small child, looking grim and angry. She shakes her head in denial now and then. When I say, "She's an alcoholic," she winces as if it is the first time she's heard me call her that. I know that what I am saying is painful for her, but I also acknowledge that I probably haven't made life particularly happy for her, either. I try to calm her rage: "I know I lose my patience with you, Mom, but you need to know that I love you and want only what is best for you."

When the social worker responds, speaking for Mom, it is evident that the two of them have spent time "talking." Mom is very good at manipulating others to say or do what she is uncomfortable doing herself. Now, Anna says, "Your mother feels overwhelmed by you. You tell her what to do. She says you're controlling her by bringing in hospice. She doesn't want anything to do with them. And when she recovers and is walking on her own, she wants to go into an assisted living situation and not live with you."

Mom shakes her head in agreement when Anna talks about my role in Mom's care. While she makes no accusations, she clearly believes I've been abusing and/or bullying my mother. Although I'm happy that Mom would like to live elsewhere, part of me is also hurt and feels betrayed. It's as though nothing I have done has been of value to her.

The discussion moves on to hospice and the fact that Mom doesn't want them involved. Anna says, "Your mother feels you want her to give up the idea of ever getting better."

I respond, "Of course I want her to get better. What you say is all well and good, but my mother has not had a chance to talk to the hospice people herself. If she decides against it after she meets with them this afternoon, we will not push it. Let's let her decide in the end."

I want to be a realist, but I don't want to say that Mom's doctor told me there isn't any hope of her returning to her former life. Under the care of hospice, she will at least be kept comfortable and will have them to help her solve any problems that might develop with the nursing home.

Someone who is not involved in the health care industry told me that nursing homes do not encourage hospice to become involved with their patients' care while they are residents in a home. Apparently, once hospice is called in, the facility has to split with hospice the money the insurance companies are paying it. I cannot prove that this is true, but it's interesting to note how dead set against hospice the nurse was last night when I told her we would be speaking with them today. Could there be a bit of greed involved in this situation?

The meeting ends with Anna telling me, "Your mother doesn't want you to visit her for at least a month." That's fine by me, and I propose that Mom and I seek family counseling, but that doesn't fly. In truth, it probably wouldn't help anyway. We've been down that road before.

OVER A TASTELESS LUNCH, BILL and I discuss the morning. It's a good thing he has broad shoulders. I complain about the busybody nursing staff and all that I've already been through. "While I'm relieved that I don't need to see Mom for a while, I'm hurt. I've been fired from my job as her daughter. What a waste these last years of caring for her have been. I can think of a million things I could have done instead. I could have been painting, writing poetry, and free of the burden that is still on my shoulders. Why didn't I suggest she go into a nursing home from the get-go? I've been a fool."

When I apologize for my rant, he smiles, plants a kiss on my cheek, and says, "You're cute when you're angry." This is exactly the kind of caring I so need and have been craving from Bill for several months now.

We go back to the facility to meet with Stephanie, the hospice social worker, and Jenny, the nurse who will be in charge of her care. We gather around one of the tables in the dining room. Mom is not with us. I fill them in on what's happened since we first made the appointment with them. I let them know that we will not go in with them when they meet with my mother. I also tell them that if she decides she doesn't want them involved, we will have to go along with her decision. "I won't be happy with that, but there is nothing else I can do," I tell them.

These two women fully understand the situation we are in,

and even though I warn them that they have a difficult sell ahead of them, they're confident that Mom will make the right decision for all of us. They tell me, as so many others have, "You need to start caring for yourself before you can care for anyone else. If she agrees, we'll monitor your mother's medication and visit with her several times a week. If difficulties with the facility arise, we will do the work of getting the problem resolved. We will check in with you on a regular basis. And you can call on us any time you need to."

They also explain that there are family counselors at their office who are available to help whenever I feel like I'm losing my mind. This is exactly what I need to hear. I want to keep my crazy she-dragon from causing more problems. She exhausts me, and I can't always stop her from making mincemeat of the world. I want to learn how to deal with conflict in a healthier way.

While they are talking with Mom, I pace back and forth. She will begin rehab in the morning, and I worry she won't cooperate with the physical therapists. In fact, I seem to have "unending-worry disorder." My shoulders are tight. I mindlessly eat a whole plate of oatmeal cookies the facility always puts out for visitors, and every now and then I feel tears welling up. I try breathing deeply, emptying my mind, but anxiety wins ten to nothing. An hour goes by, and I'm getting more nervous by the minute. My stomach hurts, and I'm sweating. I feel as though my life is on the line. What will happen if Mom refuses to work with hospice and I have to continue dealing with the nursing home on my own?

When the hospice team emerges with good news, I cry in relief. My shoulders drop to their natural level. They tell me,

"She has already signed a new 'do not resuscitate' order." Stephanie and Jenny have informed the staff that they will be involved. I don't need to do anything but say good-bye to Mom and go home.

When we go in to see her, Mom is still angry with me. When I bend down to kiss her, she pushes me away. I am the safest target for this woman who is suffering so terribly and is extremely frightened. When I tell her I'll see her in couple of weeks, she snaps, "Don't rush back."

I leave without saying anything more. I try to ease into the rest of my day. It's warmer than it's been since fall. I watch several scrawny robins working the lawn in front of my house, looking for worms and whatever else they can find to help them get through the rest of the cold winter.

# 22

## SEESAW

*February 2007*

MY MOTHER'S INSULTS ARE SLOWLY HEALING. AFTER having not seen her for almost a week, I find my edginess beginning to soften. I'm building a list of things I've been ignoring. Cleaning out the fridge and doing laundry feel like major chores, but they're the beginning of a cleansing that is long overdue. Clearing clutter from a closet or two will be next. I like the feeling of spaciousness that opens up within me when I discard things I no longer want or need. I'm back at the gym and enjoying Pilates class after several months of having had no energy or time to attend. I also take naps and am sleeping better at night.

Bill visits Mom on a daily basis. After three or four days of my absence, she tells Bill, "Send Joan my love and ask her to bring me some magazines to read." I ignore the request. I'm feeling stubborn. I've been her lackey for too long. Why should I jump every time she needs something? Her last words to me were "don't rush back." Well, damn it, I'm not going to. I send Bill back with a stack of books and magazines for her.

A few days later, she calls me. "I'm so sorry for the fuss I made. I miss you. Please come visit me" are the first words I hear when I pick up the phone. I'm quite shocked. It's the first time in my memory that she has ever apologized to me for anything. And she actually admits she made a fuss. Her usual way is to forever forget the nasty discussions we have and the problems she causes. I wonder if someone, like Bill, has been coaching her. I tell her I'll stop by tomorrow afternoon.

Are we on the mend? One part of me says yes; another says, *Be careful. You don't want to go jumping back into the stockpot that you were drowning in just a week ago. You're on firm, dry ground now. Don't go losing your footing*. But curiosity and guilt get the better of me, and I cave.

When I visit Mom the next day, I see changes. She's lost some weight. Her arms and legs seem stick-thin. Her eyes are sinking into her skull. But her color is good and her attitude is much better than it has been. Her smile is huge when I walk into her room and hand her a box of her favorite chocolates. She giggles upon her first bite of a dark-chocolate bonbon, stuffed with creamy caramel and a hint of cinnamon.

But seeing her physically failing in such a short period of time gives me pause. I'm feeling sorry for my disdainful thoughts about her, and I can't help but have compassion for her suffering. Despite all the talk of her healing and being able to walk again, it's clear that she really is dying. I sometimes forget about that in the heat of our battles. When I leave to go home, it's a tearful moment for me—life is changing, and fast.

Bill and I are planning to visit our daughter and grandkids next week. And in just a month or so, we'll go off on another trip, to Yellowstone National Park, to spend time wolf-watching. We sent our money in to reserve our spaces for that trip last summer, long before life got overwhelming. Now I'm worried that we'll have to cancel the trip if Mom starts going downhill.

When we arrive in North Carolina, Lisa reports that Mom called her a few nights ago. "It seemed like a good-bye call," she reports tearfully. Mom told her that she just wanted to say that she loves them all. She chatted with both Zoe and Noah, and afterward, when they handed the phone back to Lisa, Mom was very weepy. Lisa has always adored both of her grandmothers; for her, they've provided examples of strong women who made their own way in the world. I'm beginning to think I've been swimming against the current, because I don't feel that way about them. I see giving in to alcohol as giving up. It's also occurs to me that maybe I haven't presented myself as a strong woman for Lisa because of my obvious struggles with anxiety and depression. But I refuse to be someone I'm not. I hope that my own strength shows in my wanting to change and bring peace into my life, rather than hiding myself in a liquor bottle.

When we return home, we discover that Mom has canceled her daily newspaper delivery. When the physical therapist told her that she needs to sit in her wheelchair for at least an hour every day, Mom refused. She said she preferred her bed and wouldn't budge. Could this be the result of our bringing hospice in?

I never know what will happen next. I depend on Bill's strength too much. Being the fixer that he is, he tries to keep me from melting down while keeping his own drooping emotional levels from public view. Though we disagree on a lot these days, I realize he can see and understand what I can't grasp as Mom struggles with life and death. I'm too caught up in my own pain and grief to see that we're all suffering together. I haven't quite figured out that I am not alone on this journey.

Even though I've been taking care of my own messes, Mom's apartment sits untouched since she went into the hospital with a broken shoulder. Downstairs and out of sight, it's waiting for someone to clean the place up, empty the garbage and her refrigerator. There are still dirty dishes in the dishwasher, waiting for someone to add soap and push the ON button. I guess that someone would be me. I don't mind cleaning up after myself, but picking up after Mom right now is another story. Her leftover presence in my home makes me feel enslaved. Her dirty dishes continue to chain me to the decision I made when I asked her to live with us.

An argument with Bill over my not wanting to clean up the apartment turns into an exchange of loud curse words and blame. Bill gets in the car and leaves for an hour. Trying to control my anger and desperation, I call the counselors at hospice. They listen patiently and compassionately as I sob into the phone.

On the worst days, my stomach flutters painfully if anyone shouts at me. I try to take cover, but there's no place to hide. I think about what it must have been like for US troops on the beaches at Normandy. They were dropped onshore, caught in the open with the Germans firing at them. They couldn't go back into the sea. The only place they could go was forward, through the grenades and gunfire. They either lived through it or died. If they managed to get through to the other side and go home alive, they were more than likely to experience severe psychic trauma.

Again, I contemplate how it would feel to shut it all out. I imagine a deep, dark, quiet sleep. I wouldn't hear or fear the grenades. I wouldn't hurt any more. But I know I need life to march ahead through this war. My thoughts shift to what I want to do once Mom is gone and I can breathe again.

I begin seeing Dana, the therapist whom the hospital chaplain recommended. She takes me through guided meditations to get me relaxed. Within a few weeks, I come to realize that all I can do is rise each morning and live from moment to moment. Life is what it is. There will be good days and bad days. I can choose to make the best of every moment or I can mark each day off one by one, as I kick and scream myself into oblivion.

Dana gives me homework. "Ask yourself at least a dozen times each day if you are doing what you feel like doing and if it makes you feel good. If it doesn't, you need to change the situation." She adds, "Don't see your mom more than twice a week."

During the next month, Mom is up one minute, down the next. Bill and I are riding the same roller coaster. Then, suddenly, Mom is spending up to three hours a day in physical therapy. She shows me an ad in a magazine for a rain jacket she'd like and asks me to order it for her. I guess she hasn't given up after all.

As she heals and begins standing for short periods of time, the facility warns us that she will soon need to leave. She will have to go either home or into an assisted living facility. But she isn't walking yet and the head physical therapist says, "I'm not done with her. She needs to be using a walker before she can leave." I've heard that Mom has been feisty lately with the staff. It sounds like her will to live is back, and I wonder if the facility is trying to kick her out because they're tired of dealing with her and her bitchy daughter. Finally, hospice weighs in and we get the home to agree to give us more time.

Bill and I visit three assisted living facilities in the area. We choose one that is particularly homey and just down the street from where Mom is now. There's a small indoor pool and a large library, and on each floor are large birdcages with canaries chirping, greeting us as the elevator doors open. It's neat, clean, and run by local folks, not a corporation somewhere out of state. A small apartment will be vacant in about a month. It has a little living room, a kitchenette, a bedroom, and a bathroom and will be thoroughly cleaned and repainted.

We push Mom over in her wheelchair to check it out. She likes it; she seems excited by the friendliness of the residents she meets and responds to their welcoming words with smiles and words of gratitude. In the hallway, she talks to the canaries as if they are parrots and will respond to her once they get to know her.

When Mom begins using a walker, I act like a proud parent cheering her on. But it's all a show. I know the facility will want to release her very soon and worry that it will be while we're away. Her new apartment isn't ready yet.

At the same time that Mom is moving forward, I'm falling backward into old patterns. Every minute of every day is filled with things that needed doing yesterday. Trying to recapture the time I've lost dealing with Mom, I stupidly sign myself up for several beading workshops. I know there is no time for that. We're leaving for our ten-day trip to Yellowstone in just two weeks. Unfortunately, hospice is in the midst of change. We have a new nurse and social worker to get acquainted with. That will take time. I liked the other ones better.

Mom is complaining of pain in her shoulder, and not much is being done about it. I'm staying behind the scenes, letting her take it up with the facility and hospice. I feel extremely selfish, but I'm slowly beginning to listen to those who are encouraging me to let go.

As I run myself into the ground, I melt down over and over again. I panic when I can't get it all done. There are tears, tantrums, and crazy behaviors that I'm terribly ashamed of. I'm being just like Mom, insisting that things be done my way or no way at all. I've often been told that I look just like her and have always taken that as a compliment. She was a beautiful woman. But now, when I look in the mirror at my own graying hair and the wrinkles beginning to show, I hate what I see. I don't want to look like her, never mind act like her. Why did I sign up for this gig? When will this craziness end?

BACK FROM YELLOWSTONE, WE HAVE five days to move Mom into her new digs. She's excited. I bring her back to her old apartment so that she can choose which pieces of furniture she'd like to use in her new home.

Mom enjoys the lunch I've prepared for her: a grilled cheddar-cheese sandwich on my homemade bread, and freshly prepared tomato soup. Now that she has a walker and is fairly mobile, we promise to have her back for dinner whenever she feels up to it. She oohs and aahs over the garden just greening up and the river silently slipping by. She talks about taking her cat with her, but Cleo spends most of her time outside. She'd have to stay indoors all the time if she went with Mom. Sadly, when Mom came in, Cleo didn't seem to remember her and ran off down the hall, looking for a hiding place. Later on, when she finally came out, she hung back and wouldn't let Mom touch her. It's heartbreaking to watch. I can't imagine how I'd feel if one of my beloved pets didn't recognize me after being apart from me for a few months.

On top of that, Mom is shocked to discover that Bill has moved his office into what used to be her living room. His old office space was cramped and in the garage. In winter it was a cold, wet walk back and forth. Here, even with my mother's sofa and armchairs, he has more space for his desk and file cabinets. He repainted the room sage green and replaced some of Mom's wall art with posters of plays he's acted in or directed. And her old bedroom has been rearranged, as we now use it as another guest room.

It's an awkward situation. Kind of like a first-year college student coming home for Thanksgiving to find his or her bedroom has been turned into mom's sewing room or dad's "man cave." The look on my mother's face makes it clear that she is a bit taken aback and suspects Bill and I are happy to be rid of her. She's right that we're happy, but that doesn't mean we don't feel guilty about taking over her space. Still, it's simply time for all of us to move on. We try to talk to her about it, but she changes the subject every time we bring it up. What started out as a happy reunion in her old home has turned into a hurtful affair.

Getting back to business, she looks around and whispers, "I don't want to leave any of it behind." But her new space is quite small compared with what she had here, and there isn't room for most of it. In the end she decides to take her huge desk, her favorite shabby recliner, her television, and a small, glass-topped patio table she'll use as her dining table. I suggest that she rent a hospital bed, which can be raised or lowered and will therefore be easier for her to get in and out of, but she retorts, "I do not need a hospital bed, thank you very much! All I need is my regular bed. I'd like to get back to living a normal life, you know."

A week later, Mom is settled in her new digs. I sit back and take a break from the chaos. I want life to be like it was before Mom moved in with us. But as I laze in the sun, seated in my favorite armchair, I slowly begin to panic as I look ahead. I still have laundry to do from our trip, and unpaid bills are piled high on my desk. There are those beading classes I signed up for in a moment of insanity before our trip. The garden is calling; it's time to start seedlings for the vegetable garden. I have packets of seeds for several varieties of tomatoes, sweet peppers, eggplant, broccoli, and spinach. There are directions on how to build a worm farm awaiting my attention, and the invasive kudzu taking over the riverbank will need to be cut back once longer days and warmer temperatures bring on its growth. I've been considering the idea of growing potatoes in large bins, like a friend of mine did last year. Then there are the perennials I need to thin and move to fill in empty spaces.

I'm way ahead of myself. All of my crazy intentions are bringing on feelings of being overwhelmed and the usual gnawing-away of my stomach. I'm living on adrenaline, caught between fight and flight, not knowing where to go. It's been six years since Mom moved in with us. Those years have slowed my pace; what used to be easy to manage in one day now takes two or more.

I thought my life would resume where it left off, back in October 2001, before Mom spent her first night in the apartment downstairs. I don't really know what I was thinking, but life isn't like a series of television shows that we can tape and save to watch later, when we have time. It keeps on going, regardless of our efforts to stop it in its tracks.

During these past six years, billions of gallons of water have passed by the riverbank we live on, trees have fallen in storms, pets have come and gone, and my own face has begun showing its age. Nothing is what it used to be. The path I once followed is overgrown and impossible to find amid the thicket of time.

# NEGATIVITY *and* NARCISSISM

*March 6, 2007*

MOM TURNED EIGHTY-FOUR TODAY. WE HAD LUNCH with her in the dining room at the facility and shared an almond-flavored birthday cake I preordered. The meal was a casserole of chicken and rice, accompanied by steamed asparagus and a tossed salad. Despite Mom's continuous complaints about the food, I found it delicious. The other residents sang "Happy Birthday" along with us as she blew out the candles. Mom smiled and nodded grandly, like a queen waving to her people.

She's still complaining of shoulder pain, and the new hospice nurse, Jean, and social worker, Bev, are spending more time with her. They've increased her dose of morphine to keep her comfortable. When they suggest that she would do better in a hospital bed, she agrees and remarks, "Why didn't Joan think of that?"

They give me a call every few days and lately have reported that Mom is being extremely difficult. She's telling stories that aren't true. They go something like this: "I told Joan to stay away for a few weeks because I need my space." In truth I told her, "I'll give you a few weeks to get settled in before I spend a lot of time with you. I have lots of stuff to catch up on at home, and it'll give you time to get to know new friends and neighbors." She's been telling tales like this for years now, and I find it difficult to keep myself from wanting to make the truth known. But I'm learning to be quiet, and that it will do no good to correct her. I think she truly believes what she says.

Though I returned from our trip fully rested and eager to get on with life, I'm back to feeling exhausted and have difficulty getting out of bed every morning. When my eyes are barely open, the "dreads" take over my mind. I ask myself, *What can go wrong today?* My list of annoyances has expanded, and occasional pains in my lower back are telling me I have a kidney stone. I try to ignore all of it, but in the end I freak out. I have no time for that now, and add my own health to the long list of worries and plans I make in the wee hours of most mornings, as if I can control any of it.

Mom usually calls me once or twice a day just to talk. Too often, it's when I'm in the middle of doing something. Though it's annoying, I do my best to be patient with her and share what's going on here at home. One late afternoon she calls to tell me that the facility handyman has arrived to install the full-length mirror that Bill bought and dropped off at her place only a day ago. She whines, "Bill neglected to leave the screws we need to hang it." My dear husband is out, and I tell her to check all surfaces and the floor in case they fell or rolled into a corner.

I have a feeling they are right under her nose. Two minutes later, she calls me back screaming that she still can't find them. She wants the screws "now!"

Pissed off, I stop peeling potatoes for dinner and load myself into the car. I need to see what I can do to ease another daily Mom crisis. En route, I try calling Bill. Fortunately, he answers his cell phone and says he can't get away right now but tells me where he left the "damn screws."

When I walk into Mom's apartment and point to the screws on top of the glass patio table, she responds, "Well, you could have told me." I want to say, *Go fuck yourself, Mom*, but I leave without uttering a word and wonder if I'll be like that one day when my kids are trying to help me out.

As I try to walk out the door, she rants, "The food is bad. The vegetables are overcooked, and the meatloaf is the worst I've ever had. My laundry comes back wrinkled, and they're always losing things." She has it in for everyone, but the chef is at the top of her list. When I stop at the front desk to ask for their take on Mom's behavior, I'm told she announces loudly, to everyone in the dining room, "What a lousy cook. The spinach has the green cooked out of it. I wanted chicken soup tonight, but all he has is his nasty onion soup." She has told the supervising nurse that she wants to organize and dispense her own medications. She argues with Jean, her hospice nurse, about it and complains she's exhausted from all of the visitors she's been hosting. But Mom hasn't had any visitors lately and is often found pacing up and down the hallway outside her room, as if looking for someone to talk to. Is her dementia getting worse? Or is the extra morphine causing this dysfunction?

When I drop off the groceries I buy for her every couple of

days, I don't stay long to visit with her. I can't stand her negativity, which often wipes out the positivity I work hard to maintain. It's more difficult than ever to be around her, especially when she starts telling me, "I hate this place. Why did you put me here? I want to go home. I have no friends here, and you're no help at all." Bill tells me not to take it personally, but I can't seem to figure out how to do that. I'm trapped. I've been a victim for too long, I guess.

Mom calls one morning to say that her friend Doris will be bringing her by the house so that she can pick up a few items of clothing that she needs. I tell her I'd be happy to bring them to her, but she says, "No, no. It will be good for me to get out."

When they arrive several hours later, Mom is all gussied up in an elegant dress that reflects the blue-green of her eyes. She's wearing matching open-toed heels. She's a true clotheshorse and has always dressed to the hilt. Her lips are smeared with bright red lipstick, and she has rubbed more onto her cheeks. Her smile is broad as she shows her friend what Bill has done to her apartment. She's giggly, like she's been sipping something strong, but I don't smell any alcohol on her breath. I ask if I can help, but she waves me off and, in a sweet six-year-old voice, says, "I can do it myself." I hold my breath, worrying that she'll fall as she pushes her walker along the stone pathway out in the yard.

She reminds me of a clown or a little girl parading around the house playing "grown-up," wearing her mom's clothes and high heels that are way too big for her. But she is a grown woman in her eighties. At first I find it funny but then become alarmed that she isn't being herself. I've never seen her like this before. Who is this woman? Has she reverted to her childhood?

I help load a box of clothes and knickknacks into the car, and as they pull out of the driveway I fall apart, unable to accept that my mother is no longer who she was. I don't know how to deal with the strange apparition that just stood in the doorway.

I'm so disturbed that I call my therapist, Dana, to tell her I need to see her before our regularly scheduled appointment next week. "This experience with my mother is too surreal. I don't know how to handle it. Between her storytelling and her performance here today, I'm feeling as though I've been turned upside down and am walking backward. Is it me or is it Mom who is living in a state of delusion and self-deception?"

When I finally meet with Dana, she reminds me to think about it all in a different light. "Yes, your mother's dementia is getting worse. She's on a larger dose of pain meds, and her thinking is very clouded. The hospice people are doing their job, keeping her as comfortable as possible. She continues to lose weight and is having more difficulty breathing than ever before. She *is* dying. It probably won't be long before she's gone. And it will probably be a blessing for both of you."

Dana suggests that Mom has a tendency toward borderline or narcissistic personality disorder. It's just a label, but it explains a lot, especially her lies and her dismissal of everyone who tries to help her. As the term "narcissism" implies, it's an overboard sense of self-love and importance, probably caused by the abuse and lack of love Mom experienced as a child. Her mother was most likely a narcissist, as well as her grandmother.

Dana says that I am a co-narcissist. Like other children with a narcissistic parent, I naturally feel as though I'm selfish and bad, and that the only problem in my relationship with Mom is me. I have deferred to her point of view simply to make things easier for myself, and as a result have allowed her negativity to become mine. I have lost my ability to express myself in a healthy way. Dana reminds me how I hate confrontation and that my low sense of self-esteem causes me to defer to Mom and anyone else who has an opinion that differs from mine. In adapting to who she is, I have allowed Mom's sense of self-importance to thrive and have allowed my own sense of identity to diminish.

After our talk, I feel a slight sense of relief. But I have lots to think about. If my mother, grandmother, and great-grandmother were narcissists, does that mean I am, too? I could certainly say yes, sometimes, like when I feel deserving of special attention and treatment because of the time I've spent trying to do my best for Mom, then being the recipient of her vilification. Or when I allow my dragon to take over my being and become demanding. I also think about the times when I pushed back and hurt my mother in return for her treatment of me. Was I being evil, or was I simply trying to take control of my own life in an unhealthy way?

I obviously have to keep working on my own recovery and building a healthy mind. Now that I see Mom and myself more clearly, I understand my own need to get out from under her influence. No wonder I've been ambiguous in my care for her, loving and hating her at the same time. And there are my continuing problems with anxiety and depression. Who wouldn't be losing their mind?

Dana suggests I visit with Mom only when I can take someone else to accompany me. She believes Mom won't show her nasty side when other people are around. She hugs me and says, "There is nothing to be done except to keep your distance." She also provides me with the titles of several books that she thinks would help me to further understand what is going on. The best and most readable on the list is *The Drama of the Gifted Child*, by Alice Miller.

When this is all over, I'd like to be able to walk away from the war between Mom and me without feeling guilty. I know that won't be easy. These last few years have been a living hell. Had I known that it would turn out this way, would I have invited her to live with me? Honestly, I don't know.

# 24

## SPRING

*April-May 2007*

AFTER WEEKS OF DELIBERATION, MY BROTHER REID IS on his way to visit us. I haven't told Mom he's coming. I didn't want to get her hopes up and then see her be disappointed if he didn't show up. She'll be happily surprised, I'm sure.

He arrives on a beautiful April morning. The forsythia hedge in the front yard is bursting with yellow blooms that glow through the half inch of snow that fell overnight. It's a wonderland, two seasons colliding in all their glory. Having driven most of the night, he's just in time to witness the magic before the sun melts away the night's fluffy white frosting.

I'm hoping there won't be any family squabbling while he's here. I yearn for his help and want him to be involved in Mom's care, even if it's only for a few days. I want him to know what it's been like for Bill and me. I've had no help whatsoever from either of my brothers since this journey began. I need at least one of them to understand the responsibility I've taken on. Reid's being here will give me time to attend to my kidney stone problems and the surgery I have scheduled in a few days. I need to get that fuss out of the way.

Reid and Mom have always had a special bond, despite their frequent battles over work and money. Over fifty years ago, when my mother found out she was pregnant with Reid, her doctors told her that this child would most likely not reach full term and that she was putting her own life in danger. Her blood type clashed with my father's, hers being RH negative and his being RH positive. At the time, there were rarely difficulties with the first child and parents often didn't know there could be a problem with later pregnancies. Their second child, who was born when I was two or three years old, died within days of his birth. That's when Mom and Dad were told about the problem and were advised that they should not tempt fate by trying to bring another baby into the world. But they apparently weren't careful enough, and a few years later, when my brother Zed was born, he was termed a "blue baby" and spent a long time in the hospital before he was stabilized and could come home.

Four years after his arrival and nine years after mine, Mom found herself pregnant once again. Not willing to give up the pregnancy, she decided to go as far as she could with it. Surprisingly, Reid made it to full term but was close to death. The doctors performed a miracle and were able to save him. As a result, Mom took special care of and interest in him. He was obviously her favorite child. There was an understanding between them that Zed and I weren't privy to.

Reid was an adorable baby and toddler, with deep-blue eyes and platinum-blond curls. Just looking at him melted my heart, and any jealousy I felt toward him faded. I cared for him when Mom was busy, and it was often my bed he climbed into when a sudden rainstorm brought thunder, lightning, and winds that frightened him during the night. Sometimes I felt as though he were my own child.

In his early years he could do no wrong, but in his teen years he became a rebel, part of the hippie generation that couldn't put up with their parents' consumerism and political beliefs. After Bill and I were married, Reid moved in with us. It was a good thing for a while. He and my father clashed continuously, making life intolerable for both of them, as well as for the rest of the family.

When my son, Mark, was born, Reid moved back home to finish his last year of high school. With a baby of our own, Bill and I could no longer direct our attention to Reid. He found the competition difficult, and our once-close relationship began to weaken. And after he married, it came to an abrupt end. Our frequent phone calls to each other became rare on his part, and when we did speak, he was distant and icy. I felt as though he was getting his revenge on me for having my own child. His relationship with our parents also fell apart, and they rarely spent time together, even though they lived in the same community. Mom felt abandoned, as if she had lost another son, and Dad was angry that Reid never finished college and preferred to squander his time, and what money he earned, on growing pot and practicing his newfound love, blues guitar.

After Dad died, Reid stayed away from Mom, visiting her only when he needed something—usually a meal or money.

Knowing what I know now, I suspect that Reid, like Mom, also suffered from borderline personality disorder. He has also shown signs of paranoia, occasionally calling me in tears and telling me that people are trying to kill him. When I ask who they are, all he'll say is that they're his enemies and that he's afraid for his life. I've spent a lot of time worrying about him, but by the time Mom began living with us, I had no time or tolerance for his problems. He has always wanted more than I could give him. I've felt used and abused by him, and I know Mom feels the same way. Though she complains about his taking advantage of her, she is constantly forgiving his neglect, providing him with whatever he needs. In return for her generosity, he rarely calls her, and last month, on her birthday, he neither called nor sent her a card.

But for right now, everyone's rough edges seem to be smoothed out. Mom is excited when Reid shows up unannounced to spend time with her. He takes her to lunch, and then they go sit behind the facility, beside the pond where she has been going to smoke. He rolls his own, while Mom puffs over-the-counter brands. She's been smoking less than she was before. Despite her worsening cough, the words "lung cancer" have disappeared from all conversation with her. But with Reid, who has his own addiction, she seems to be trying to keep up with him. At this point, though, I don't suppose it matters how much she smokes. It's too late for her to quit and find her way back to health.

Mom and Reid talk and talk until they can't talk anymore. It's nice to see her happy and to see them getting along so well. Mom tells Reid all the things she's been keeping from Bill and me. For one thing, she is terribly upset that Bill moved his office into her old living room. "I just don't understand why he had to do that. He had plenty of room up in the garage."

She also tells him that she wants to come home to live because she hates the facility she's "stuck" in. He seems to understand and asks Bill and me to talk with her about it. When I do, all I can find to say is, "I don't think it would be healthy for us to live together again." Feeling very uncomfortable about this discussion, I follow that with, "There is no way I can have you back in my house. It would only make an already horrible situation worse."

Bill, always the diplomat, tries to counter my comments, pointing out the huge number of pros versus the few number of cons surrounding her staying where she is. He talks about how we all squabble when we're together for too long, and she admits, "You're right. I was terribly lonely before I went into the nursing home."

Besides all that, I, too, am enjoying having Reid here. He's between wives at the moment and is wondering if he might like living in Virginia. He's reaching out for something that is difficult to find—an end to his suffering. We tour him around various communities he might feel comfortable getting to know. He spends evenings out at the area's numerous music venues, thinking he might find a place for himself, but in the end, he says he'll stay in New Hampshire, near his son. His first grandchild is due to be born next month.

After a week and a half, he begins to understand what I've been going through with Mom. He tells me, "I get it now. I haven't asked her for anything. I just wanted to visit with her. I don't need to be reminded about what she's done for me." He's angry that she started haranguing him about getting a job and putting aside money to pay his own taxes. Now he regularly receives dunning notices from the feds about his income taxes, which he rarely pays. Trying to stay neutral, I tell him, "Yes, I know. It isn't easy to listen to all of her complaints, especially when they're about us. Sometimes I think that she's waiting for us to be what she wants us to be before she decides to die."

Tired both emotionally and physically, Reid continues to visit with Mom every day for a few minutes, until he's had enough. I stay out of their way, letting them battle through their own issues. A week later, Reid says farewell and is on the road back to his life in New Hampshire.

In the meantime, my stuck kidney stone has been removed. I'm supposed to rest, but if I lie down for a nap, all sorts of worries come to mind. Being busy keeps my demons away. So I buy more plants and work in the garden to keep the darkness from taking over. The harder I work, the more exhausted I become. The number of plants yet to be put in the ground grows every day. I'm obsessive-compulsive about plants and my need to have the world's most beautiful garden. It's part of the emotional storm that I can't shake. Bill begs me to stop overdoing it.

A week or two passes, and Mom announces she wants to move to another facility. She still rants about the food to the chef, and now none of the staff is left out of her temper tantrums. She causes so much trouble, I'm afraid they are going to tell me she has to leave.

Bill and I know from all of the research we've done that there is only one more possibility to check out. They invite us to bring Mom for lunch. When we do, she is smitten with the place and wants to move in immediately. But they don't have a room for her and it will be at least a month before one is available. I know she's scared. She wants to feel secure and safe. I think she believes a new place would be just the ticket to keep her alive. But somewhere inside her confused and failing mind, she knows that she's simply waiting for the end. It breaks my heart to watch her suffer like this.

A few days later, early in the morning, we get a call from the facility telling us that Mom awoke at three in the morning, having difficulty breathing. She's been taken to the ER, where she is being given steroids intravenously to open her airways. I go to see her. She tells me, "I'm tired of the pain and the struggle." She is very weak. Her oncologist saw her earlier in the day and again told her, "The cancer is spreading quickly. There truly is nothing more we can do for you. Your bronchitis is probably a result of the cancer and your emphysema."

He suggests that she might want to move into Hospice House, where she would be kept comfortable for the rest of her time and would have hospice nurses and volunteers at her beck and call. She says she wants to go. Again, there isn't an opening for her, so she goes on a waiting list. But she's confused and unclear about what is happening. When she discovers that it's a place where you go to die, and that there are no field trips to the latest art openings or movies, she changes her mind. Back she goes to her rooms in the place she hates most in the world.

I've begun writing e-mails to cousins and other relatives about Mom's condition. I continue to see my therapist, not to dig through the past but simply to get through what is shaking my world at this very moment. I feel deep compassion for my mother, but I can't process my dislike for her. I'm not yet wise enough to step back and see that things are happening as they will and that I cannot save her from herself.

Mom needs more oxygen as the days go by, and the lack thereof is screwing up her brain function even more. As her brain fog thickens, it becomes more difficult to have meaningful conversations with her. She spends more time sleeping and sitting around but still seems to have enough energy to get up and use her walker to go out behind the building, where no one will catch her smoking.

During all this, Bill plans a quick trip to London to see friends and some good theater. I don't want him to go. It doesn't help that at the moment it costs less to fly to London than it does to fly to New York. He's tired of putting his life on hold. I go back and forth between feeling angry and envious that he can just leave. I'm about to be abandoned at one of the most difficult times of my life. He has some nerve. Mom is quickly slipping away, and I need a hand to hold.

We argue for days about his trip. Our continuous conflict is all it takes for me to send him packing, even though I've got more kidney stones to deal with. I'm tired of fighting. I'm tired of trying to get my feelings across to him. I accuse him of "leaving a sinking ship." But deep down I'm beginning to believe I do need to be alone. I can take care of myself. I decide to stop worrying about making him happy. Mom is being cared for. I just need to care for myself—to go to bed early and get up late. I want to cook what I feel like eating, when I want to eat it. I don't want to argue anymore. "Go," I tell him.

Days later, and a few hours after Bill is in the air, I pass another kidney stone without incident. Two more follow the next day. I spend a few hours getting the last of my "OCD" plants into the garden. I start reading a book that's on the top of the stack that sits next to my bed and take myself out to dinner.

I haven't had time like this for ages. When I'm by myself like this, I get creative. I've been daydreaming about painting and poems I'd like to write and have taken long, silent walks in the woods. I think about how nice it would be to have all of that back in my life again on a regular basis.

When I visit with Mom a day later, I sit with her for half an hour. Several of the nurses tell me that she apologized to the chef, saying that she was sorry for all of the trouble she caused him. They say she's been very calm and very peaceful. Now, she seems to have nothing more to say and just wants to be alone. I promise her I'll return tomorrow with her favorite orange sorbet, lilacs freshly cut from the garden, and the ginger cookies she loves so much. I return home, take the dogs for a long walk, and settle back into the book I'm reading. I'm living in the moment, knowing that tomorrow will take care of itself and yesterday was but a whisper.

Before I go, she asks me to call a few of her friends to tell them that she won't be here much longer. She says, "I just want the lights to go out." Five days later, they do.

# FINDING MY OWN WAY

*June 21, 2007*

IT'S BEEN A MONTH SINCE MOM DIED, AND I'M SCARED, like I was when I was about six years old and lost sight of my parents while I marched in a Halloween parade. I was dressed up as a gypsy, with a silk turban on my head and a long, frilly skirt that swept the leaf-strewn street. I was accompanied by Cinderella, Sleeping Beauty, a few dwarfs, lots of witches, and ghouls and goblins. All of us kept our eyes on the sidewalk as our parents followed along, trying to keep up with us while maneuvering through the crowds who were throwing candy our way. When I stopped to pick up several pieces and then stood up to make eye contact with Mom and Dad, they were gone. They weren't where they had been just a few seconds earlier. I ran to the side of the street, looking desperately for them, but I couldn't break a path through the bystanders.

When a fireman, dressed up in his uniform, saw me sobbing, he took my hand and led me to the place where the parade would end. It took a few minutes to find my parents, and when I finally spotted them, I ran to them, crying hysterically. They laughed at me and continued talking with their friends, never taking my tears seriously or knowing just how afraid I was.

I'm feeling the same kind of terror now, at sixty-five years of age. As crazy and dysfunctional as we were, when my father died, I still had my mother. She gave me the family connection I needed. Now Mom is gone, I'm completely on my own and the oldest in my family of origin—the matriarch, someone who is supposed to be filled with wisdom and all knowing. I'm parentless, an orphan. There is no one to check in with and get advice from, good or bad. Am I ready to grow up and be my own, independent person?

Even though the shackles that held us together are broken, it is difficult to let go of her. Mom was the one on whom I could blame my own dysfunction. Now I have to come face-to-face with it on my own. I fear that looking into the mirror and seeing beyond an aging face will be painful and take me back to my beginnings, where I don't want to go.

On the other hand, now I have a chance to discover who I really am. It's time for me to reexamine where I've been, the consequences of my choices, and where I might be headed. In addition to my relationship with Mom over the last seven years, there are other issues that I must look at carefully. I need to assimilate all of the broken pieces of my existence into one. Life will go on, even though I'm late to my own party.

I still hate Mom for what she has done to me, while at the same time I miss her. I hate myself as well. I don't think I did a good job of caring for her. I know I was mean to her at times.

But I'm also exhausted from dealing with the grim reaper and am not ready to abandon my own life; I just need time to contemplate how I might spend the rest of my days without the stigma of being an unworthy daughter. I want to become the person I know I can be: worthy of love and able to give it back in abundance.

I've run away to an inn on the Chesapeake Bay for some R & R. My body aches. My head is filled with mist and dark clouds. I've scheduled a massage, a pedicure, and a facial over the next few days at the spa next door. Being here and nourishing my body will give me time to think through what's transpired in the past few months and where I want to go from here.

Friends and relatives have been spouting their wisdom on the mourning process, telling me how to handle my mother's financial affairs and how to make myself feel better. At any other time I might be more open to their suggestions, but right now I'm tired of nodding my head and saying thanks for advice that I don't want. I know everyone means well, but I just want to be left alone for a while. I don't need anyone to feel sorry for me.

They all seem to think I miss my mother and am grieving her loss deeply. I may be in mourning, but it isn't for her. It's for myself. I'm still in a state of shock. Like many people who have been abused, I have always partly assumed that nothing will ever change. If I'm not the victim of one form of abuse by one person, I'll experience another kind by another. Time and history build the patterns we live within. They are difficult to change, like giving up booze or tobacco. But I am free of my mother's part in directing my life. She can't make snide remarks or criticize me anymore. I no longer have to walk on eggshells in order to keep peace in my house.

But am I really free? When she died, I expected I'd be able to jump right back into painting, beading, writing poetry, and living a creative life. But it isn't as simple as surfing channels on TV in order to find something pleasurable to watch. And I know this weekend on the shore won't be enough time to fix everything. But it's the best I can do for now. Being away from home and Mom's ghost even for just a few days should help to begin clearing the downed trees and war-torn buildings that have been cluttering my mind for a long time. If I can begin the process of finding myself and ways to approach the next few months, that will be enough. For now, this is what I've got. I'm here to listen to what's going on in my head, and I need to use this time to the fullest.

I've brought my journal and a few books to read. But mostly they lie unopened on the desk. I stare into space, wandering through the twists and turns of my life: my childhood spent in helpless confusion, the gift of a loving and supportive husband like Bill, and the many choices I've made, especially concerning my mother. And there are a multitude of questions I cannot answer: Did I abuse my mother during her last years? Did she really abuse me? What is abuse? Why do I hurt so much? Am I allowed to be happy now?

I don't want to talk to anyone except to be polite. Last night in the dining room, an older couple asked me to join them. They felt bad that I was eating alone. Apologizing, I said, "No, thank you. I just need to be alone right now." I hope they weren't insulted. Today I plan on ordering my meals in my room. And if it remains sunny and not too hot, I'll sit on the lovely deck out by the pool, overhung by large, shady oak trees. It's a great place to simply close my eyes and listen to birds calling, toddlers splashing in the shallow end of the pool, and the constant chatter in my head.

The crossroads I'm at is not your usual four-corners kind of deal. It's a hub of sorts, with innumerable roads shooting off in all directions. I'm afraid I'll choose the wrong road. I know I can't stay where I am for long, and I certainly don't want to go back the way I came. But where *do* I go? And what does it mean to be free of the burdens I've spent these last years carrying? What about the torturous fear that is suddenly popping up? Has it been there all along? Is this the issue of abandonment I've always hidden and am finally rid of?

Over the next few days, as my body is touched and cared for by others without my needing to give back, much of the tension melts away. None of the body workers ask me questions, except about my general health. I have no need to explain myself, no need to ward off advice. I'm carrying around a lot of stuff: anger, guilt, and shame. My shoulders and back have especially felt the load. These healers' soothing hands are working their magic, and my mind floats free from the pain.

But after my sessions at the spa and I return to the cloister of my room, my mind goes back to all of the questions. What should I do about Mom's ashes? Social norms say it's necessary to plan a funeral or memorial service for her. My brothers are not picking up the ball and taking care of that part of this mess, and I doubt they're capable. It needs to be done right. But when I begin wondering what to do, I get panicky and nauseous. Mom is still here and won't just go away. My shoulders begin to tighten again. My neck gets stiff, and my brain goes into hiding.

Though her ashes, still sitting on their shelf in the closet, haunt me, I can't deal with them right now. To be perfectly honest, I'd rather never deal with them. I want somebody else to make final arrangements for her; there are too many other things I need to do in order to wipe the slate of my own life clean. There are relationships I need to mend, places I need to go, and experiences just waiting for me to be part of. But the fear and the "shoulds" filling my head make me hesitant. My mother's ashes need to be tended to. I've literally been left holding the bag.

## THE FIRST BURIAL

*Early November 2007*

I'M TAKING A WONDERFUL CLASS ON GROWING AND using herbs as medicine with a small group of women who make me feel wanted and appreciated. We may not agree on everything, but we have the same values and philosophy on life. We all believe in plant power and share laughter and sadness, along with supporting one another as we travel through our own lives. I'm still not quite sure which road I'm on at the moment, but it feels right. I'm beginning to loosen up and am enjoying myself more than I did a few months ago. Bill's and my social life is picking up, and I've been experimenting with new recipes and inviting others to come and join us for a meal. Once the holidays are over, we plan on making a habit of having friends over for dinner at least once a month. It's refreshing to be with people I haven't seen in long while, and the list of those I'd like to reconnect with is growing.

But I'm aware that my body is not well. I'm frequently light-headed and exhausted. I'm told I'm not getting enough rest and that I'm probably suffering from adrenal fatigue. I'm still filling my life with endless activity that keeps me from beginning the work I promised myself I would do. The herb class is helping me to discover herbs and foods that will address this issue. I need to get more sleep and to start meditating again. In the last months, I've let that go for no reason at all. My excuse has been that there are not enough hours in my days. But I'm beginning to think that getting back to a regular sitting practice would be time well spent, and would help to keep me centered and mindful and thus aware of what my physical needs are.

That I haven't honored Mom with a funeral or memorial service haunts me. I think about what I can do to bring peace back into my life. If I just did *something*, I would be more able to face the other issues that often overwhelm me.

I play around with the idea of planning a memorial service up north. Mom wanted to be buried next to Dad, in Hanover, New Hampshire. But that idea quickly flies out the window because it would be too hard to plan from a distance. When I bring up the matter with my brothers and ask them how they'd like to do it, they show no sign of being interested in launching such a project. They seem to think that since Joan has been in charge all along, why not just let her keep doing her job? I find myself getting more and more infuriated by their lack of caring about their mother and me.

I'm reminded that when Mom was still living in New Hampshire, she generously hosted a gathering of friends for Reid when his wife passed away. Reid complained to me that she had not prepared the food herself and, worse yet, had put out paper plates instead of her fine china. Somehow the feminist movement has not made a dent in Reid's thinking. Like my father, he believes that women are still supposed to do all the dirty work.

Bill kindly reminds me that he's happy to help, but there is no rush. "You can do whatever you want to, whenever you choose to do it. There really is no deadline." But I'm obsessed. I need to get Mom off my back and out of my life.

I come up with a plan for a pre-Thanksgiving affair in Virginia. We'll invite the brothers and other family down from New Hampshire and have a memorial tea for Mom, to which we'll invite her friends from this area, as well as all those who helped take care of her during her last months. I set the date for the second weekend in November and begin cooking, filling my freezer with good, healthy dishes for the big event. My family members are well known for the amount of food they can put away, so it's a long, drawn-out task.

My vision for the tea is a late-afternoon "do" with a variety of teas, spicy apple cider, and lots of cookies, which I'll order from a bakery. I don't need to add sweets to my cooking chores. It will be on a Sunday afternoon. And since my sense of humor is beginning to return and I've always been somewhat of a cynic, I arrange to have a smoke tree planted in the yard in honor of Mom. She smoked until the day before she died. We'll bury some of her ashes beneath it, along with a pack of cigarettes. She had a very dry sense of humor, and I think she'd get a kick out of that. I plan to send the rest of her ashes home with Reid so that he can bury them next to Dad. I've done enough and consider this the end of my obligations.

When the family comes together in November, we go through the usual tension. It doesn't help that Reid has brought his new girlfriend, Lynne, who seems quite nice until day two. She's a total stranger to most of us and talks nonstop, wanting to impress and be accepted by her lover's family. This gathering doesn't seem to be about honoring Mom anymore—it's all about Lynn. Thankfully, she and Reid are staying at Mark's home, so it isn't a twenty-four-seven kind of deal; still, it's more than annoying that she tries to outdo herself and make herself a member of our family.

Zed is staying with us, along with Reid's son, Jesse, his wife, Amanda, and their baby daughter, Anya, born just a week after Mom died. I've often speculated that Anya is the reincarnation of my mother. If she is, she's done a complete turnaround and come back as one of the sweetest little people you could ever imagine. I flirt with her, play peekaboo, and hold her close. We're all born tender and innocent. It's life that changes us. The slings and arrows we meet along the way leave their scars, and we're never the same as we were when we were infants. I wish I'd known Mom when she was a baby.

There is a bit of a kerfuffle over the fact that I've not prepared a traditional Thanksgiving dinner. The best I've been able to muster are simple, healthy meals like homemade chili, cornbread, coleslaw, and guacamole. Since the weather is still warm, our Thanksgiving meal will be several different salads, barbecued chicken wings, and homemade bread. But Lynne is expecting turkey with dressing, along with pumpkin and apple pies. When Reid tells her about our family tradition of making pierogis for Thanksgiving and Christmas dinner every year, she lets me know in no uncertain terms that my having not spent the required hours of preparation to make them is not acceptable. When we're alone for a moment outside in the garden, she tells me, "I'm very disappointed. I was so looking forward to a real Thanksgiving meal."

Because I've always been caught up in pleasing everyone around me, my guilt pokes its head out from the pocket in which I try to keep it hidden. It quickly turns to rage, and I hear the flapping of wings and feel the heat of approaching fire. I've prepared five days' worth of meals for my family and am opening up my home for a tea to honor my mother, and Reid's narcissistic girlfriend, whom I've never met before, wants the universe all tied up in pink ribbons? I imagine Lynne flying through the air and landing in the cold river at the bottom of the hill.

I keep my thoughts to myself, trying to keep peace within the fold. But now and then I can't help but become acidic. When Lynne tells me seriously that she expects Jesse and Amanda, who are as broke as she is, to prepare steak and lobster for her and Reid on Christmas Day, I sneer and reply, "You don't expect much, do you?"

On the day of the tea, the weather is perfect and warm enough for us to assemble outside on the deck. People who said they would be there don't show up, and those who never said they were coming do. Though everything goes well, I'm feeling somewhat intolerant after being with my extended family, plus Lynne, for four days. I'm aware that the "beautiful" smile I'm usually known for isn't genuine. I've stuck it on with glue. I feel stiff and barely able to carry on a conversation. I wanted everything to be perfect so that my guilt would fade quickly, but I'm not able to relax. I just want them all to go away.

Relief arrives the next morning when the relatives climb into their cars and return home to the North Country. I wave to Mom as her ashes exit the house with Reid and Lynne, thinking that she and Lynne have much in common. Reid hints that maybe we'll see them again in December. I wince, take several deep, cleansing breaths, and think rancid thoughts. I spend the rest of the day trying to get back to my own life, understanding that nothing is simple and that for every step forward I take in this healing process, I will take two, if not three, steps backward.

# THE HEART *of the* MATTER

*Thanksgiving Day 2007*

I HAVE NEVER BEEN SEXUALLY ABUSED, BUT MY SHADOW memories of beatings and psychological neglect by my parents when I was a child have clearly caused me to live a life filled with pain and fear. I liken my wounds to old sports injuries that I thought had healed but that suddenly return later in life. They cause me to limp and cry out in pain as I get older, and I blame them on those around me who don't see my worth.

Living so closely with my mother over these past years has opened up a memory bank that I thought I'd securely hidden from myself. But I suppose we can never truly leave the past behind. Even though my mind has created blocks to stop me from reliving what happened to me years ago, my cells have their own memories and my subconscious can hold only so many secrets before it begins to leak—especially when an abuser like my mother is continuously kicking and prodding it.

The number of memory hits that seem to come out of nowhere often bewilders me.

These old demons even affect my relationship with my husband. After all the time I've spent of taking care of my family and then Mom, I sometimes feel as though I deserve more than I've been given. Our kids have grown and gone, Mom has passed on, and I long for a more spontaneous life and a genuine partnership with Bill, but I'm feeling very confused about how I've gotten where I am today, and I think some changes are due.

While I love Bill and don't want to be without him, a small part of me longs for a place where I don't have to worry about anyone but myself. I don't want to allow myself to be abused or make so many compromises that I feel held back from living my own life. Is that how it was before Mom became ill? Is it possible to be in partnership with someone and still have a life of one's own?

Encouraged by Dana, whom I've stopped seeing regularly but occasionally talk to by phone, I've made an appointment for both Bill and myself with another therapist, who specializes in marital relationships. Dana recommends him highly and says he's the best couples' counselor around.

Bill isn't keen on the idea but finally gives in after much heated discussion. "Okay, okay! If you think it will help, I'll go." Like other men I know, he is uncomfortable talking about how he feels. He always seems surprised when I tell him I think we need to discuss personal issues. The onus has always been on me to show him that we need help in order to live rewarding lives.

When Mom moved in with us and became our focal point, everything that was important to us as a couple was put on hold. We disagreed about many things, and I often wondered if it was just because Mom was living with us or if our relationship was falling apart for other reasons.

Bill has always been all theater, away at rehearsals and traveling to see the latest shows on Broadway. It seems as though he spends much more time away these days than he has in the past. I'm discovering what loneliness is, especially during the months when he is in rehearsals on a nightly basis. I find myself waiting in the wings, wondering why. I want to reconnect with what I like doing and share some of it with him, but we seem to be drifting apart instead. Why is there no time to drive up into the mountains together and watch the sun set over the Shenandoah Valley and the hazy Allegheny Mountains beyond?

Too often when I try to talk with him about my concerns, he brushes me aside. He sometimes seems depressed, and if I say, "Sweetheart, you seem down today. What's happening? Can I help in any way?" he answers simply, "I'm fine" and continues reading the newspaper without even looking up.

A few weeks ago, I told him that we seemed to be spending most of our time apart. I said, "I'd like us to have more quality time together."

As he rushed out the door, he said, "That's fine. Figure out what you'd like to do, and I'll make time for it." I want us to plan something together so that it will appeal to both of us. I feel as though I'm butting my head against a stone wall.

When Mom was alive, he always seemed to take her side when it came to the mother-daughter issues that filled my life. I accused him of not being supportive of my efforts to get through the mess I knew I'd created by inviting Mom into our home. I want to leave that past behind, release my feelings of emptiness, and replace them with something more fulfilling. If he isn't interested in joining me on the journey, there is little I can do. But before I start the hard work ahead of me, I need to know how important I am to him.

Amid all of my wondering whether we are still a pair, I am continually confused about what I want and what role I am playing in contributing to the possible demise of our relationship. I still carry the shame I felt when Mom died; I frequently ask myself if I did all that I could have done for her. I struggle with my inability to be strong, like those who soldier on through events that are far more difficult than my own. I think that I'm too needy, and therefore mentally unstable. Why can't I just get over myself and move on, the way others do? And why do I always feel as though the world is about to end?

Playing a destructive game of "Whose Fault Is It, Anyway?" Bill and I spend several rocky weeks seeing Dr. O. We argue and blame each other for what looks like death and destruction to me and small potatoes to Bill. We're on opposite sides of the fence most of the time, making snide comments and throwing explosive insults at each other while we're getting nowhere in particular. We do have our moments of talking seriously and kindly to each other, but it's evident that Bill is not happy seeing Dr. O. "He's too much of a feminist. He doesn't hear me and what I'm saying." We quit going to him, and the dust I've loosed into the atmosphere slowly begins to settle. Bill seems less defensive and suggests that since we have no plans for the coming weekend, maybe we should plan something special, like going out to dinner and a movie or driving to Richmond to see what's happening over there. Maybe we just need time.

A few days later, I pick up my copy of *The Drama of the*

*Gifted Child.* I've already read it once, and most pages contain underlined passages and notes I've written in the margins. It's about children who are "gifted" with the ability to go numb and not notice they are being abused. Just like the kids in the book, I was too busy taking care of my needy parents while trying to find the kind of love I needed and didn't receive when I was a child. When I made my parents happy, they returned my love. But it was so hard to please them. I was like a little dog. I did whatever it took to be nourished. I would lie, cheat, or keep quiet, just for a smile or a pat on the head. When I was not being a slave to their dysfunction, I ignored the pain and physical harm they doled out and believed I was responsible when the world started crumbling around me. As children, we have only our parents to protect us, so if they fall down on the job, we have nowhere to go.

Rereading the first few chapters of Alice Miller's astounding book, I once again recognize myself in the descriptions of other adults like me: afraid, filled with shame, broken, and never enough to satisfy those who supposedly love me. I have rarely trusted those around me, and lately I haven't been trusting of Bill. It is no wonder we are often at odds. Bill is not responsible for my despair. He has his own issues, but I now see I've been projecting my difficulties onto him—just like my mother took out her rage against life on me.

I cry relief-filled tears, like a mother who has suddenly been reunited with her child after years of being apart. I am deeply grateful that Miller's book has come to my attention again. I now see that I'm grieving for the loss of my childhood and have blamed what I thought was abuse from those around me on everyone else, including my husband.

I resolve to become a whole person living without fear and hatred. I know there will be many hills to climb and that at times I'll be unable to see what's on the other side. It may take a long time to undo the damage that has been done, but as I begin to climb, I don't allow myself to look back. The only thing I see is the crest of the hill in front of me.

# 28

## THE FACE *of* DENIAL

*December 2007*

As CHRISTMAS APPROACHES, I FIND MYSELF MISSING Mom. Though I still generally dislike the holiday season, I can't quite let her go just yet. I pull out the Christmas decorations, looking for ornaments Mom made for us, like the small Christmas tree she fashioned out of a huge pinecone that she painted green and decorated with wee acorn cups filled with tiny seeds and other natural findings from the woods and gardens she frequented. The red felt mantel cover she made, a collage of antique Christmas cards, hangs in all its glory on the fireplace. Now that she is no longer ruling my life, it is easier to remember the good times I had with her, like the Christmases when we were a team and prepared for the big pierogi-making production line that included Bill, Mark and his family, and whoever else was available and would be coming to our feast.

As the holiday approaches, Bill and I relax in front of a warm fire and twinkling lights. Handel's Messiah plays in the background. We see friends and spread good cheer for the first time in years. I take solace in the fact that the burdens of the past seem lighter, but I'm still extremely anxious at times and quick to react to certain triggers I don't yet understand.

Bill and I seem to be back on solid ground, enjoying each other's company. We spend Christmas Day by ourselves. Our kids are off doing other things. Best of all, Reid and Lynne have decided to stay in New Hampshire for the holidays. I don't need another crazed family Christmas to look back on years from now. Since it's a sunny and unseasonably warm day, I work in the garden, trimming back last summer's dead flowers. It feels like the beginning of a cleansing ritual.

During my annual checkup with my nurse-practitioner in January, I fill her in on the details of what has been happening and how anxiety still tears me apart. She strongly suggests that I see a therapist who specializes in treating trauma. It's the third time a member of the medical community has told me that I suffer from PTSD. I can't fight the diagnosis any longer. Aware that I need help, I call the doctor she refers me to. I don't want to continue living in fear and angst and hating myself. Nor do I want to make life difficult for those around me. I do not want to be like my mother.

The first time I see Dr. M., I'm impressed. She's elegant, very Southern, and a bit older than I am. Unlike one or two of the therapists I've seen in the past, who became friends of mine, she's extremely formal. Though she scares me a bit and at times reminds me of my mother, I'm anxious to find a new road through life and believe someone who doesn't become overly involved with me will be more helpful than someone who "likes" me and feels sorry for me. After I answer her questions about my general moods and behavior, we agree to begin work the following week. I'll see her on a weekly basis until we agree that I need to see her more or less often.

As the weeks pass, I find it almost impossible to answer her prying questions. She wants to know everything about me, including my relationships with my husband, kids, and friends. I feel shame and blame for all of the awful things I've been through in my lifetime. I don't want to be judged by someone I'm not yet sure I trust. What will she think of me if I tell her what she wants to know?

Thinking I've made a big mistake, I consider not going back to see her. But something I can't identify keeps me returning each week. Finally, on a warm spring day, when I can't hold back any longer, my pain slips out onto the floor in front of me. I break out in loud bursts of sobbing. I feel uncontrollable rage. I want to throw and smash everything around me. I leave, telling myself I need to find someone else to help me. I hate this woman and wish I were dead.

But I go back the following week, at our appointed time, with my tail between my legs. I apologize profusely and begin telling her some of what she wants to know. I've been in denial for so long I don't know what is true anymore, and I let go of the fear of hearing the things that pour out of my mouth and onto the table in front of us. When the session is over and I see that Dr. M. isn't judging me, I feel lighter and ready to dig more deeply into what has been keeping me so tied up in knots.

Over forty years ago, after Mark was born, I suffered from postpartum depression. Probably sensing that I might have other issues as well, the psychiatrist I was seeing at the time asked me, "What are you so afraid of?"

I answered, "I don't know. I don't think I'm afraid of anything." His diagnosis led me to believe I had a chemical imbalance within my body due to my pregnancy. He assured me that taking a pill would fix the problem and make my depression go away. I had no inkling that my upbringing was far from normal and that hidden within the walls I had built between myself and my past, there were major storms brewing. His query has stayed with me, and I have often asked myself that same question in the midst of a panic attack. Perhaps now I'll begin to find an answer.

Years later, in a writing class I attended, I was given an assignment to write a story about my past. I couldn't do it. There was nothing there to write about. I explained to the teacher, "I seem to be running on empty and can't come up with anything."

"That's okay," she said. "Just write about what you are feeling right now." I must have written something, but all I remember is disliking the teacher and the class with a passion. It's amazing how well the brain keeps its secrets. But now things seem to be loosening up and changing.

So how and why does someone pack away her childhood and forget about it for more that sixty years? I don't really know, but somehow I managed to do exactly that. Did I not hear the loud banging from the locked trunk I stashed under my bed over the years and completely ignore it? I was good at hiding the hurt my cells remembered. I dazzled everyone with a gorgeous smile, looking like I had a handle on life. But the happy look wasn't real. The pain and sadness were always there, and, unbeknownst to me, they were calling me to make some repairs.

I remember the time ten years earlier when I was cruising through a secondhand/antique shop looking for bits and pieces of "stuff" I could use in my collage work. Among the tables overflowing with old postcards, ancient magazines, and collectable stamps, I spotted a large doll sitting on a red velvet chair, staring at me. She was old and broken. I swear she winked at me.

She had long, stringy blond hair. Some of it was tangled and hung in tight frizzy curls. She looked like she'd recently had a partial perm that went bad. I noticed a few tiny bald spots where her hair had pulled away from her scalp. Her face was covered with a network of tiny cracks, and her teeth were chipped and looked sharp. Her glassy blue eyes looked out into the world with an emptiness that broke my heart. She'd obviously been around and had been played with, hard.

After checking out the rest of the shop and finding nothing of interest, I returned to her. Though in many ways she looked like something out of a horror film, there was a sweetness about her. She reminded me of someone or something, but I didn't know who or what. Unable to leave her behind, I brought her to my studio at the McGuffey Art Center, where I was a resident artist, working mostly in photography but spreading my wings with collage, paint, and handmade books. I called her Doll, and, wearing her ragged dress, she sat off to one side of the room on a shelf.

She became my muse, inviting me into her world to play with her and a dozen or so other cast-offs I soon began to collect as part of a family of distressed dolls. Most of them were old and broken to the point that they were missing limbs, perhaps an eye, or even most of their bodies. There were doll's heads with no bodies at all. Some were intact but had a lost look about them. I even found a life-size mannequin, complete with several wigs. I dressed her in my own clothes, a feathery hat with a dark veil, a boa, and junky jewelry. Arranging these creatures in a variety of poses, I began photographing them using an old Polaroid camera.

As the camera expelled the pictures, I used a variety of tools, like discarded pens that I pressed against the surface of the image, to manipulate the fluid emulsion between the layers of film, creating blurred edges and wavelike patterns. Each one-of-a-kind print had a surreal quality in which reality and imagination came together. In many ways, the dolls in my photos looked more distressed than they really were. I was so taken with this new work that I stopped working on a series of paintings I'd been putting together for a show.

I then rephotographed the small prints and enlarged the resulting images into thirty-by-thirty-inch Ilfochrome prints for a solo exhibition entitled *Playing with Dolls*. It was hung in early 1998. Some viewers walked through the show, examining the images slowly and closely. Others walked past them quickly, seemingly repulsed by what they saw hanging in front of them. Though a few of the photographs were playful, most were evocative of fear, anger, and suffering. Oddly, several women came to me privately afterward to tell me they still had their childhood dolls and played with them often. They seemed to be happy that they'd found another doll-friendly person.

I caught a friend or two looking at me strangely. I think they supposed I'd gone mad. I reassured them, "I'm fine and having fun." But the dolls possessed me. I made up stories about what their lives had been like and the horrors they had gone through. I felt deep compassion for them and sometimes found myself singing quietly to them, trying to soothe their pain.

At the time, all I knew was that they were alive for me and had stories to tell. In the written statement that accompanied the exhibition, I wrote, "Viewers may react to the *Portraits* as a series of Rorschach ink blots. The images may evoke scenes from horror movies, early memories, and feelings of fear, anger, or sadness. They are, after all, explorations of the shadows that surround each of us and are mirrors of the soul."

I believed I was telling the dolls' stories, until one day I realized that within the images, they were playing out my story for all the world to see. They allowed me to come face-to-face with my own fears of abandonment, disintegration, and aging, as well as my trembling inner child, hiding in a world of abuse. They were teachers and healers.

But, as seriously as I might have taken them, I moved on to different work, forgetting for a time the lessons they had imparted. It wasn't until much later that I realized that they helped me to begin integrating some of the fragments of my own broken life into a whole. I'm aware that the exhibition was a call for help. I will also add that subconsciously I may have been trying to yank my mother's chains. She had just recently moved to Virginia to be near me. As her health deteriorated and my mixed feelings about her intensified, I became the good-daughter doll with the cracked face and unkempt hair, trying to come to Mom's rescue.

Denial—like fear, joy, and happiness—is part of being

human. It's a component of change, and hopefully brings growth. When we are in great pain and suffering, the easiest way to feel better is to erase the hurt, pretend it away, until a later time when we're more able to deal with what ails us. When we slowly begin to get used to whatever is pushing us into rejecting the truth, we relax a bit. The suffering returns, but it's not quite as hard-nosed as before. If we're very lucky, we eventually see our situation as it truly is and take the actions we need to cope with whatever is haunting us.

Whether it's war, physical abuse, a fatal illness, or an earthquake resulting in a tsunami, bad things abound. They're all part of our entry into the inevitable school of life. Hard times teach us valuable lessons. They are extremely difficult, and if we flunk a class, they'll be back to haunt us until we get it right. I'm sure I'll be working on my lessons forever.

If you were to ask me what my most important life lessons have been, I'd tell you that I have learned that I must use my own oxygen mask before helping others with theirs, that my heart tries to hold more of the world's pain than it can, and that I am not the worthless, broken idiot I once believed I was.

I'm learning that I have limits. That I am a highly sensitive human being who needs more space, time, and quiet than others. I need to say "no" more often than I say "yes," and despite my occasional wishes to end it all, I love life more than anything else.

I've also figured out that I am not supposed to be a first responder in every calamity that comes along. I'm supposed to wait until the pain subsides a bit before I go in and give the first responders some support.

Though I slide backward from time to time and find myself

putting on my victim cloak, I know that I am only a victim of myself.

I can still lose my temper. I can still be mean and thoughtless. I can still whine and complain. But I'm getting better at catching myself and better at making amends. I know I can't expect others to follow the same path that I'm on, and that I can't remake the people around me just because I think there is something wrong with them.

I'm learning to accept whatever I am dealt and to love and forgive myself no matter what, even if it's very hard. I'm beginning to greet each day with a smile and to live it as if it were my last. My hope is that when my time to go down comes, I'll depart gently, without regrets and without blaming anyone who didn't see things my way.

# 29

## THE SECOND BURIAL

*November 27, 2008*

IT'S SNOWING. THE WIND WHIPS AROUND ME, UNABLE to make up its mind about what direction it wants to come from and where it wants to go. My long wool coat, hat, gloves, and scarf aren't enough to keep me warm. I'm no longer used to New England winter weather. The temperature is somewhere in the low teens. But the wind chill makes it feel like it's down in the single digits, if not below zero.

I'm in New Hampshire, standing beside my father's grave with Bill, my brothers, my nephew and his wife, and little Anya—the people who were at my home for Mom's memorial tea last November.

When I sent Mom's remaining ashes home with Reid, I hoped that he'd scatter them in her favorite places or even plan an informal burial service. But he hasn't done anything with them and most likely never will. He's aged tremendously since I saw him last. He's nine years younger than I am, but he looks nine years older. His always-thin body is now almost skeletal, and he constantly complains about being tired.

We're here to spend Thanksgiving with our New England family. Not wanting to cause a rupture, I've been working on how to keep myself from reacting to Lynne. We haven't seen much of her since we arrived, and I stay as distanced as possible. She and Reid visited with us last spring, and even without the rest of the family around, she made their weeklong stay anything but pleasant. When they arrived and I took her down to Mom's old bedroom, where they'd be staying, she said, "Well, I would have thought you would have cut a bouquet of flowers for our room," as she peered out the window into my garden filled with daffodils.

Though it isn't easy, so far I'm doing well. In an hour we're expected to be at her home for a big turkey dinner with all the fixings. Since I didn't pull it together last year in Virginia, she's out to show me how it's done. I've "kindly" offered to help, but, thankfully, she wants to do it herself. She'll get extra points in somebody's book for that, I'm sure.

But for the moment, we're here out in the cold to bury the rest of Mom's ashes next to our father. Reid has brought the ashes and a spade to dig the hole. This is actually what Mom said she wanted shortly after she was diagnosed with cancer. "Don't buy me a plot. It's too expensive. Just dig a small hole next to your father's grave and dump me in." Right now I'm thinking, *Well, sure, Mom, but the bag of your ashes is larger than a gallon-size food-storage bag and the ground is frozen solid.*

Reid and Jesse manage to cut a small rectangle of sod out of the ground. The hole is about an inch and a half deep and five or six inches wide—not large enough to take all of her remains.

I urge them to make haste, as what we are doing is illegal. A permit is actually required from the town to bury remains here. Usually, the funeral home takes care of that detail; today, we're it.

A few other cars pull into the cemetery. Each time one comes through the gates, we stand tall around the grave, hiding the shovel as best we can. We hope we look like we're praying. Actually, we're all laughing hysterically. I'm worried that my aging bladder won't hold out until we're done.

During a brief lull in the traffic, we scoop some of Mom's ashes into the hole and cover the spot with the frozen sod. No longer laughing, we stand around the site in a circle, holding hands. Each of us offers a few words to send her off. I'm sure several of us are thinking, *Good riddance.*

Jesse promises he'll take the remaining bag of ashes home and volunteers to order a small plaque to put next to my dad's, with her name on it. Perhaps during warmer weather, we'll return and scatter the rest of Mom's ashes nearby.

This cemetery was one of my mother's favorite haunts when she was alive. During the rainiest of the summer months, this place always seems to produce a large variety of wild mushrooms, including morels, the mushroomer's Holy Grail. Places where they are found are secreted from the rest of the world forever. Mom was one of the area's wild-mushroom experts before she moved to Virginia. She once told me that she knew which mushrooms were edible just by looking at their auras. She said, "The poisonous mushrooms have very colorful ones, while those that are edible are always surrounded by white light." There were always dishes of deliciously prepared wild mushrooms on her dinner table. To my knowledge, no one ever died or got sick from eating them. It seems fitting that she should be in a place she found such pleasure in.

Happy to be out of the cold, we follow the procession of cars to Lynne's house, a lovely old farmhouse on the west side of the Connecticut River, in Vermont. The central room, where the banquet she's prepared is about to take place, is huge and furnished with large tables. The aroma of roasting turkey fills the room. My stomach grumbles.

I watch Reid and Anya playing together and wonder if he will have the chance to watch her grow into womanhood. Will he be around when she's twelve, sixteen, twenty? Reid was a big part of my son's childhood, teaching him all sorts of boy things. He encouraged Mark's huge respect and appreciation for the natural world.

Around the table, Lynne is the center of attention, and even though she tells a litany of unending jokes to entertain us, a certain seriousness pervades this holiday gathering. I know that part of her problem is my presence here. When she is being overbearing, Reid catches my eye and winks at me, letting me know he understands my position.

The poor guy is caught in between his sister and his girlfriend, who loves him to death. She is very important to him. She is the one who keeps him going, tells him what to do, and, when he's feeling low, gets him to change his attitude. She is very much like a mother to him. He's always needed a strong woman in his life, and right now she's it.

As I watch this holiday scene before me unfold, I think about my concept of family. There is my "storybook family," and then there is this family, seated around the table. The first is a dream in which we all adore and are kind to one another. I've always been envious of families like that. I've spent a lifetime trying to see my own family in that light, only to feel betrayed when it never worked the way I wanted it to. Here, sharing a meal, are those who are connected by blood and another who is a newbie to these hallowed grounds. Though there is a story here, it is nothing like the pretend one. It's the real deal, made up of imperfect individuals, each spinning his or her own tale.

For me, reality is like a huge slab of marble. I've tried to chip away at it in order to create that ideal family. But I am not a sculptor. I'm unable to bring out the image I "see" in the stone —my desire and longing for perfection. Whenever I think I'm getting close to releasing it, the image disappears. Before too long, I'll chip away all of the marble, which will then lie in bits and pieces on the ground. There will be nothing left to work with. Trying to glue it all back together is impossible. I ask myself, *Would it not be better to learn to work with what I already have than to destroy it altogether and wind up with nothing?*

Like any other family, we do have our good times. Why not revel in those, rather than in the dark side of our story? I cannot remake anyone into what I want them to be. But I can learn how to be with them and accept them as other human beings who are as hung-up as I am. In beginning to slowly let go of Mom by scattering her ashes here and there, I'm letting go of the idea of perfection, not only within my family but within myself. I'm letting go of who I used to be.

We return home to Virginia a few days later, leaving Mom's remaining ashes in New Hampshire. I've not yet caught on that it is up to me, the one with the largest emotional investment, to take them with me and to continue letting them go in my own way. Still a bit too fuzzy in my head, I don't see that this story hasn't yet ended.

# FINDING COMPASSION

*January 2009*

As I WADE THROUGH THE CONFUSION AND MIXED feelings I have about my mother, my biggest question is why my hatred for her was so much more intense than it was for my dad. Her abuse was more quiet and subtle than his, and she seemed more in control of herself. She rarely, if ever, laid a hand on me, but she did lock me out of the house at times. Once when I was in college, she chased me around the house, trying to hit me with a broom for something I had done to anger her.

But our history goes way back. When I was ten or so, she taught me how to clean house, checking my work by wearing a white glove and running a finger over the surfaces I had just dusted. If a speck appeared on her clean glove, she yelled and made me start all over again. It wasn't until later that I'd discover that her mother had trained her to be a maid, as a way to put food on the table. I'm sure her mother inspected Mom's capabilities in the same way Mom inspected mine.

But most disturbing to me is the fact that while she often seemed to be my ally, Mom never protected me from my father's rage and beatings. When Dad was not at home, she made fun of him, laughingly calling him King Kong at times. But when he was around and began his inspections or punishments, she disappeared and never had anything to say about what he did. Whose side she was on? Why didn't she stop him when I screamed for her intervention? When I complained about Dad, she rarely had much to say, except that some men needed a whipping post. Apparently, that's what I was.

The rest of her behavior wasn't always exemplary, either. Once, while shopping for shoes in a discount store, she found a pair of shoes that were decorated with beaded clasps that snapped over the toe end of the shoe. They could be used with almost any pair of shoes. Not wanting to purchase the shoes only for the clasps, she tucked them in her purse when no one was looking. I saw her do it. We walked out the door without paying for them. I thought about the time when I was very young and stole lipstick from a five-and-dime. Mom made me take my loot back and apologize for stealing. She chastised me, saying, "Stealing is a sin. Don't you ever do anything like that again, or I'll tell your father and he'll take care of you." As we walked back to the car from the shoe store, I didn't have the courage to remind her of her own words. And her threats to tell my father about things that I had done always stopped me in my tracks.

I didn't understand how betrayed I felt by Mom until after my father died. Once, while I was visiting with her in New

England and having dinner with her and my brothers, Reid brought up his memories of how Dad had beaten us. Mom got upset, refusing to believe that he had ever done such a thing. She didn't have dementia at the time, and we never did convince her that Dad had indeed hit us until we were black and blue. After that conversation, I spent a long time obsessing over the idea that she didn't remember that her own children had been so horribly abused. It took a while for me to understand that she was blocking out events that must have been traumatic for her as well.

In other people's eyes, it often looked as though Mom and I had a close relationship. There were moments when I thought we did. After my freshman year in college, I took a year off and went back to Long Island to work and to try to figure out what I wanted to do with my life. During that year, I began to court my mother by sending her gifts of jewelry and perfume. I hoped they would please her, and that she'd be proud that I was earning my own way. I desperately wanted her love and approval.

But when I went home for Christmas, I recognized for the first time that she had a drinking problem. She got pretty rowdy at a party we'd been invited to and argued with my father afterward, accusing him of flirting with another woman. Now I was an adult living away from home; things were not so easily hidden from me anymore, and I began to notice her drinking behavior more frequently.

At the time I had the naive idea that if you truly loved your family, you could easily give up booze without a problem. To my way of thinking, her drinking was a sign of rejection. It was years before I began to understand that alcoholism is a disease.

The woman who would become my mother-in-law was also an alcoholic. My struggles with her taught me all I needed to know about booze.

IT WASN'T UNTIL MOM MOVED to Virginia that I began to understand the life that she had led as a child. I had known that she didn't go to school because she had to work, and that she lived with her grandmother for a while, and that her relationship with her mother wasn't close. But I didn't know all the horror stories then. Maybe I just didn't listen carefully enough.

Just before she moved in with us in 2001, I asked her to record her story for the family on a DVD. I wanted to know more about the details of her life. I thought making a recording would help me to fully understand who she was, and help her find some peace as her life wound down. We both felt it would be a wonderful reference for her grandchildren one day. But shortly after she made the DVD and moved in with us, her health declined even further. At the time, I was too busy trying to hold our lives together to fully digest what she had said on the DVD.

Three years after her death, while packing up for a move to a new home, I found a remnant of Mom's past in the form of a well-worn high school yearbook. Her name was written on the inside front cover. I set it aside, wanting to examine it more closely later. Once settled in my new home, I opened the cover of *The 1938 Record* and started turning its pages to see what they could tell me about my mother.

It was filled with notes from friends—freshmen on up to seniors—who mentioned her sweetness and wished her good luck in life. When I tried to figure out which class she was in, I found no sign of her in the freshman, sophomore, or junior classes. Knowing she had never graduated from high school, I knew I wouldn't find her in the senior class. But then I noticed that the eighth grade was included in the book. As I scanned the group photo, there she was, standing in the back row, a good head taller than the rest of her classmates. Her name was included in the list of students under the photo.

I did the math. She was born in 1923. The year printed on the cover of this yearbook was 1938. I was stunned. She was fifteen years old when she was in the eighth grade.

Overtaken by deep sorrow, I understood why she had hidden her past. I had never put the puzzle pieces of her life together. She was ashamed that she never finished school. She had to work as a maid instead, and by age sixteen she was on her own, working in a lace factory. She was like so many of us who have been abused, hiding who we are and taking the blame for the misdeeds we have suffered.

Still trying to put the pieces of her life together, I watched her DVD over and over again, hoping to find anything I might have missed, especially about school. But there was nothing to add to the picture I had in my mind.

Knowing this one little fact about Mom's school attendance changed the way I saw and felt about her. I wanted to reach out, hug her, and tell her that she was not a lesser person because she didn't graduate from high school. I'm sure my father's behavior toward her at times made her feel terrible as well. No wonder she envied me, a college graduate with a loving husband and a free, art-driven life. I can understand her bitterness. She never had a chance.

But Mom was not dumb. She compensated for her lack of education and knew how to survive. She educated herself by reading books and through hands-on life experience. Few people ever knew about her lack of schooling. She could carry on a business or political conversation with the best of them. And if all else failed, her beauty and smile captured most everyone's heart. She was gorgeous and she knew it. She often bragged that she resembled Lauren Bacall.

If she ever had a dream of being anything other than a mother, it was early on, before she married my father. She once told me she did dream of being a model. She must have struggled to find out how a beautiful young girl, living in poverty, without an education, could make her way onto the front covers of popular fashion magazines. Though I know she loved my dad, I believe she married him because it was the only way to escape from the endless pit of poverty she was living in.

There are so many questions I would like to ask her now. I wonder if things would have been different between us had she been more open and forthcoming about her life.

But there are no answers. I can only leave them to my imagination. I am certain that forgetting the ugly parts of her life was the only way she could live with herself. She was stuffed to the gills with pain, frustration, and hatred. She could not be anything other than who she was. Through her example, she taught me how to survive in an abusive world.

I, too, have hidden away parts of my life, unwilling to allow past events to determine who I am. I am her clone. I think we fought each other for Best in Show, but always tied for the blue ribbon in the categories of Perfectionism and Which One Of Us Had It Worse.

# LETTING GO ... AGAIN

*February 2009*

ALL IS WELL UNTIL I'M SLAMMED WITH THE NEWS that Reid has esophageal cancer. He's had a hard time swallowing since Christmas and has lost well over ten pounds since I saw him in November. He put off going to a doctor, but when he finally went, he was immediately diagnosed. When they implanted a device so that he could get food down, they found a stage four tumor close to where the esophagus enters the stomach. He'll spend the next few months doing chemo and radiation and fighting for his life.

I want to go see him, to cheer him on. I hear whispers in my head—*Not now. Wait*—but still I consider it. On the phone, he sounds tired and distant. He doesn't seem to want to talk about this new issue and tries to reassure me that this is just a glitch and nothing to worry about. He must know that esophageal cancer is one of the bad ones and that it has a very low survival rate, but he sounds as though it's no more serious than a severe winter cold. Lynne flippantly points out that "he'll be shoveling out the driveway the next time it snows."

I feel somewhat scorned by their curt answers to my questions and concerns. Reid is my little brother, and our once-close relationship and my memories of mothering him when he was small are apparent in my obsessive worries. So, instead of calling him too often and feeling as though I'm annoying him, I talk with Jesse and Amanda several times a week to hear the latest news. Jesse often accompanies his dad to the doctor's office. He says that his father's diagnosis is no surprise to him. "My dad has been living on cigarettes and caffeine for years. He brought this on himself." Jesse and Amanda have a spare room and are encouraging Reid to move in with them. But he chooses not to, instead seeking respite with Lynne, who is eager to help. But we all worry that she isn't taking the situation any more seriously than he is.

When his doctors prescribe major surgery "to remove as much of the tumor as possible," I know it's bad news. I believe in being positive in all things, but Reid and Lynne's continued dismissiveness about the whole scenario seems ridiculous to me, and I can't separate myself enough from the situation to accept their frivolity. It doesn't occur to me that this is the way they have to play it if they're going to get through what's ahead.

Whenever I do try to call Reid, Lynne answers the phone and is in control. I feel as if I've already lost him, and I sometimes wonder if Lynne is trying to keep him to herself. It is common knowledge that she is jealous of his former lovers, and perhaps she's jealous of his family as well. On the few occasions when I do get to speak to him, Lynne puts the phone on speaker so that she can do most of the talking.

Anger and humiliation begin to accompany my feeling of being rejected by him, especially when I remember his sometimes irresponsible behavior toward our parents and me in particular. Before Mom was diagnosed with her cancer, he disappeared off the face of the earth for several months, never returning Mom's frantic calls. Finally, in tears one afternoon, she screamed, "He's dead! I know he is. He would return my calls if he were alive." She asked me to call the police in Meriden, where Reid lived. She wanted them to go to his house and check on him.

I made the call to get Mom off my back, but I resented the fact that she wouldn't do it herself. I spoke with an officer who said he knew Reid personally but hadn't seen him in a long time. Calling my brother an "unusual character," he agreed to go out to Reid's home to see if there was any sign of life. An hour later, the officer called me back. "Reid is home and was outside splitting logs when I got there. He seems fine and said he's been busy with his snow-plowing business. I told him that you'd called me and suggested that he call you because you were worried about him."

Two hours later, Reid called, grinding me into the dirt like a cigarette butt with the heel of his boot. "Why did you call the police? Do you know what that does to my reputation? What I do is my business, not yours." I tried to explain that Mom was worried about him, but he continued to tear me apart. I hung up on him when he wouldn't listen to what I had to say. In tears, I found myself hating both Reid and my mother. I promised myself that this would be the last time I'd ever get caught up in the middle of somebody else's toxic insanity. In time, that wound scabbed over, but the injury never fully healed.

AS THE WEEKS PASS, WHEN I do manage to talk to him, Reid sounds weak and exhausted. I begin to see how Lynne is so like my mother. Both strong and controlling, they were all about themselves and how they wanted things to be done. Reid has always needed women to lean on and has chosen to ignore his own decision-making abilities. If Lynne doesn't want him to talk with me, he doesn't. He's exchanging his own power for the love and attention he gets from Lynne. I'm just getting over dealing with my mother's last years. I don't want to go through a similar scene with Reid.

A month later, Bill and I go to New Hampshire to spend a few days visiting with Reid after his surgery. He's still in the hospital, and the seriousness of his condition is suddenly catching up with Lynne. She tells me, "Preparing liquid food for him and then having to pour it into a tube plugged into his stomach is not what I signed up for. I'm trying to get my house ready for his return, and I need to move furniture around and bring the bed downstairs. I don't know if I can get it all done in time." When I ask if we can help, she quickly says, "No, I'll do it myself." All she seems to want is pity and recognition for her martyrdom. We return home ahead of schedule, knowing there is nothing we can do for either one of them.

AFTER REID HEALS FROM HIS surgery, he is diagnosed with a heart condition. He and Lynne spend the next few months traveling and visit Mexico for a few weeks. He buys an old, beat-up mobile home, planning to fix it up for their next adventure. But though most of his tumor was removed, the cancer has begun metastasizing throughout his body. His heart begins to give out, and, after a stroke and an attack of appendicitis, he slips away at home while Lynne, a few friends, and his son sing and play the blues to send him off.

It is difficult for me not to be there with him, but before he makes his exit I am able to tell him that I love him and will miss him. He doesn't need me there, crying and making it harder on him, as he spreads his wings and flies off into the night.

THOUGH I SEE PROGRESS IN my growth, I easily slide back into old ways: complaining, being a victim, and critical of everyone and everything around me. I'm more aware of my own behavior than ever before, and I believe I should be able to stop my anxiety and panic attacks on a dime. I beat myself up when I can't, and find myself taking out my frustration and anger on everyone, including the checkout girl at the grocery store who made a mistake ringing up my purchases and a mailman who is late delivering an important package I expected earlier in the week.

I'm easily triggered by the innocent words or the appearance of someone who looks like one of the people I find it difficult to be with. Once, while I am swimming at the local gym, a man who looks very much like my father gets in the pool. I panic and fill the rest of my swim time, which is supposed to be a calming activity, with fear and thoughts about someone I don't even know. By the end of my workout, I am aware of the problem and marvel at how easily I can be prompted to experience anxiety.

There are lessons around every corner, and every person with whom I have contact has a role in my life as a teacher. Especially the most difficult ones—like Mom.

# CHANGING LANES

*June 2010*

I'VE SPENT YEARS BELIEVING THAT I'M A BAD PERSON, a pain in the butt, who is overly sensitive and unduly emotional. I believed I was broken. I was often depressed and anxious and had panic attacks. At times I believed that my work in art and writing was a waste of time. That I saw a therapist and took medication to manage my anxiety and depression filled me with shame. The knowledge that my grandmother was mentally ill haunted me.

I've embarrassed myself with my crazy behaviors and have felt especially bad that Bill has had to put up with me. I've worried about what my kids think of me; perhaps they see me as a sometimes overwrought and controlling witch. I've had difficulty making friends because I feel unworthy of their attention and companionship, often afraid that they would find out that I am damaged. Does that make me mentally deficient?

Although I continue to experience confusion about who and what I am, my ability to discern the difference between being broken and being a human being with difficulties, just like everyone else, has taken hold. I recognize that my PTSD is not a result of something that I did. It happened to me. I did not cause it. It is a result of years of emotional abuse. Every cell in my child's brain and body took it as it came, transforming it into an uncontrollable security system, making me vigilant at all times.

Living in misery is not what I want for the rest of my life. There must be a way to stop the sirens and gongs that go off in my head when my brain detects danger ahead. I've tasted too many good days, and I know that every day can be filled with joy and love. I know that I have choices, but bringing about change is not an easy thing to do. My inner critics, whose voices sound just like my parents', tell me I can never recover. *You're not worthy. You aren't strong enough. It's not worth it. It'll take the rest of your life to get there.* Tell that to someone as stubborn as I'm told I am, and it becomes a challenge.

With the help of my therapist and the support of my husband, I'm working hard. I'm beginning to see the difficult people in my life as human beings trying to do the best they can, just like me. I'm discovering that judging other people does not help me to find the joy I seek. I try imagining walking in somebody else's shoes, envisioning what their lives must be like. I'm listening more carefully to what people are saying. I am more aware of words and expressions that can send me off the deep end, even when they aren't meant to.

I'm doing a number of things to keep myself calm and balanced. "Self-care" is my new byword. I'm learning to pay attention to how my body feels. Aches and pains can be indicators that something is wrong and not necessarily caused by a sprain or physical injury. The feeling of having a boulder in my stomach tells me I'm anxious about something. I often get pain in my neck when someone I don't like much is aggravating me. I'm beginning to recognize my limits. Everyone has them. Why did I think that healthy people didn't need to set boundaries?

I've quit trying to be like everyone I admire, or to be who others expect me to be. I can only be myself—a highly sensitive introvert who has had some unfortunate circumstances in her life. It's getting a bit easier to say no to things I'm not comfortable doing, instead of saying yes and suffering the consequences.

Still, it's hard to accept who I am at times. I really want to be like everyone else, enjoying parties, huge crowds, and noisy celebratory events. But when I try being part of those things, I find myself frustrated and exhausted trying to keep up with what's going on around me. Violent movies and stories make me very tense and fill me with pain. Comfort and happiness for me are light comedies or love stories, filled with characters experiencing personal growth. Uplifting endings are essential.

It is important that I understand I have choices, such as taking action if I'm uncomfortable. I'm learning to recognize feeling overly tired or unsafe in any situation. If I'm scared, I back off and choose another way to do what is before me. I've stopped hanging out with people who make me feel uneasy. Knowing my triggers helps me to avoid nasty situations.

At the same time, I'm trying to stay open and take risks when I feel curious and adventuresome, which can be quite often. Besides learning about what to avoid, I need to learn that hiding away in a dark cave will never be the answer to my suffering. Of course I sometimes make mistakes. At other times I'm surprised by the joy and feelings of accomplishment I get doing things that might be scary at first. Traveling alone, all by myself, is one of those things that, though not always comfortable, I take great pride in.

One of my biggest difficulties is the fact that I've been taking Paxil for the last nine years of my life. I began taking it before Mom moved in with us, trying to get my depression and anxiety under control. Always in the back of my mind are the addictions within my family of origin. Mom was an alcoholic, and my brothers were addicted to alcohol and lots of other substances. I don't want to be like them. I want nothing to do with addiction. That I *need* an antidepressant to keep my brain healthy mortifies me and makes me feel weak, addicted, and unable to be who I want to be. I do recognize that it did help me get through those last, murderous years with my mother, but I'm determined to leave it behind. I pray that I can live a happy life without it.

I return to the psychiatrist who prescribed it for me and, at his suggestion, begin weaning myself off the drug. He tells me it will take a while, but I'm impatient. I want results now. A month or so later, I forget to take it for a number of days and feel great. I decide to go cold turkey, believing I can do this myself without going off gradually. But a few days after that, I'm suffering and in pain. I experience extreme dizziness. Out of nowhere, I hear loud, unexplainable, explosive sounds. I have difficulty sleeping because of my extreme anxiety and have little energy to do the simplest tasks.

I go online to read about Paxil and discover that other

people have had the same symptoms and difficulties even when they slowly wean themselves off the drug. I revisit my psychiatrist, who apologizes profusely for having prescribed it for me. "I never realized how addictive this drug is when I began prescribing it to my patients. It is a very difficult drug to let go of. And I'm not the only doctor who feels that way about it."

When he suggests I start taking it again and then begin the weaning process all over again, I refuse. I am scared of what is happening to me. I am addicted to a little pill in a bottle. I'm ashamed and fear it will be the death of me. I don't want to extend my dependence on it. Right or wrong, coming completely clean seems like the only solution for me.

I soldier on through what seem like endless days. A few months later, the dizziness is mostly gone but I'm still anxious and often depressed. I find it difficult to focus on anything. At the same time, Reid's imminent death and our being in the middle of moving into a much smaller home aren't helping. I feel as though I am losing my mind. Most nights I fall asleep around three in the morning and wake an hour or two later. The dizziness returns, and my brain feels fogged in. I don't know what to do, but I know I need to do something radical to get myself out of the deep pit I'm trying to crawl out of.

Crazy as it sounds, when I hear about a writing workshop in Taos, New Mexico, taught by Jennifer Louden, a friend and mentor of my daughter's whom I've heard wonderful things about, I sign up immediately. I need to get away. I need to write about what is happening to me. I've been to New Mexico by myself before and found it a spiritually refreshing place. Without a doubt, I know that going there will help me in some way.

Two weeks before I am to leave, I go to my family doctor for a checkup and to discuss my extremely low energy levels. After a quick look at me, Dr. K. wants all the details of what has been happening. When I tell her that I am sleeping only two hours a night, she tells me, "You shouldn't be going anywhere. Unless you start sleeping eight hours a night and get yourself back on track, I'm telling you to stay home." I tell her no to taking sleeping pills. She insists that I go back on another drug that will help with my over-the-top anxiety and depression. I again say no. She replies, "Pride is getting in your way. Some people need help to live a peaceful life, because of chemical imbalances and the toxicity their bodies hold. There should be no shame in taking care of yourself. The side effects of the drug I want you to take are nowhere near those of Paxil, and it will be easier to go off it should you want to try to be drug-free later on. Let's just get you healthy again."

Exhausted, scared, and at my wits' end, I give in. I start taking another antidepressant/anti-anxiety drug, along with an herbal sleep remedy. My first night in Taos, I have my first full, eight-hour sleep in well over six months.

Being at the workshop is the best thing I could have done for myself. The new drug is helping, I've ventured out of my comfort zone, and I'm not afraid. I have ample time to myself to write. The other participants, all wonderful women, are willing to share themselves with me. My mind is abuzz with new ideas, and I can't seem to write fast enough. The word "memoir" starts popping up in thoughts and conversations.

After my week in New Mexico, I return home changed in some way. I feel better about myself and have made new friends who aren't disturbed by my still slightly fearful demeanor. My confidence is returning. My thoughts are clearer than they've been for a long time. I've rediscovered the freedom I so love when I go out into the world by myself. Spending time with people I don't know and experiencing cultures other than my own are absolutely necessary if I'm to recover from my trials. Though I still have a long way to go until I can wring out my dirty laundry completely, I've let go of a number of burdens in the desert Southwest. I feel lighter, closer to being myself again, and ready to tackle whatever will come next.

# CANCER *and* JOY

*August 2010*

TWO WEEKS AFTER I ARRIVE HOME FROM NEW MEXICO, I notice a few bloodstains in my underwear. It happened once or twice this past spring, but when it stopped, I never thought about it again. But now I'm hearing messages from somewhere inside my brain that it's not to be ignored. I swing back and forth between *maybe I shouldn't worry about it* to *I'll wait another week or two*. But it continues on and off. I'm way past menopause. This shouldn't be happening.

The word "cancer" is everywhere—in the pages of a magazine I read as I wait for my car to have its oil changed; as the key element in a book I recently glanced through; and in today's newspaper, in a front-page article on cancer statistics and promising new treatments. I know these are all signs.

Before I even call my doctor, I'm imagining worst-case scenarios in my head. I have cancer. It's terminal. I'm following in my parents' and brother's footsteps. I'm scared. I don't want to die. Everyone in my family dies of cancer. I've always assumed I'll go the same way. Why am I surprised? I'm just not ready. There is still too much work for me to do.

The story I'm writing in my head gets even more drawn out, and I'm working myself into an impossible state of anxiety. I find it difficult to focus on anything else, much less decide what to cook for dinner tonight or what clothes to put on in the morning. I'm overwhelming myself with sadness and worry.

I attend a group meditation and dharma talk by the local insight meditation community. The evening's topic is how we bring suffering upon ourselves by inventing stories about whatever is bothering us. Instead of taking action and feeling positive that all will be well, I've been procrastinating, afraid of what I might learn, while listening to the negative chatter in my brain. I do it all the time. My stories are most often tales of disaster and the end of the world. Why do I insist upon living in a made-up world, paralyzed by fear?

Convinced I need to take action, I call my doctor the next day and make an appointment. She's very kind and supportive and tells me that most likely there is nothing to be afraid of. Even in worst-case scenarios, there are treatments that will help me live a productive life.

The results of my pap smear come back, showing abnormal cells present in my uterus. My doctor sends me to a gynecologist for further testing. The new doctor recommends that I get a biopsy, which will be more specific. It's scheduled for the next week. I'm told it's an easy procedure. I'll be in and out of the hospital in a few hours, with little to no discomfort.

I stomp out the new story lines that want to take shape in

my head. I'm scared out of my mind, and it's hard to live just one moment at a time. Bill is a huge support. He goes to all of my appointments with me and holds my hand when a wave of fear knocks me over. He's afraid, too, but we try to keep all of our thoughts positive. I take the advice a friend passes on, to sit with my demons and let them be. If I acknowledge and accept them, their power over me will slowly diminish, as will my fear. It's extremely painful, but I try.

From the results of the biopsy, I learn that I have stage one endometrial cancer. "If you have to have cancer, this is the best kind to have," the doctor tells me.

I counter, "The best kind to have is none."

The standard treatment is a hysterectomy. If all of the cancer can't be removed, I'll need to undergo radiation therapy to take care of the rest. My gynecologist sets up an appointment for me with an oncologist at the university hospital. I stomp my feet like a two-year-old. "I want to go to Martha Jefferson, because it's private and has a better reputation. I've dealt with teaching hospitals before. I want none of UVA Medical Center."

What I really envision for myself is natural healing with herbs, food, and exercise. I've never been fond of doctors or the medical community in general. They've given me bad advice at times, and I've observed the damage they can do with drugs and unnecessary procedures. But everyone tells me that cancer can't be treated with herbs. Undergoing surgery is the only way to resolve this problem. It takes some convincing, but I give in. Martha Jeff doesn't have the equipment or the specialist to do the arthroscopic surgery, which is less invasive and done with a laser. They tell me that my recovery time will be cut in half and that my body and I will be grateful in the long run.

At the hospital to have some blood work done and to meet the oncologist who will do the surgery, I'm a nervous wreck. The grounds of this medical center seem like a big city to me. It's too big. There are too many people. I feel claustrophobic. I start sweating, and tears threaten to let loose. A panic attack is coming on. Adrenaline is rushing through my body. The waiting room where I sit, ready for my blood to be taken, is mobbed with others awaiting their turn in the lab. This is also where relatives who have someone in surgery congregate, ready to be called the minute their loved one is in recovery. This is not your typical TV-show waiting room, where families gather without others being present and the doctor comes out of the ER, either with a smile or without one. Here, it's all done by phone. I think about Bill's having to sit here and wait to hear about how I'm doing after my surgery.

I find the noise of constant PA announcements maddening. There isn't a seat available that isn't surrounded by other people also waiting to be attended to. I need my own space. I try to slow my breathing and keep repeating, "Relax—everything will be fine," but I want to turn around and go home. Bill gently squeezes my hand, letting me know I'm not alone.

Fifteen minutes later, my blood is filling a small tube held in place by a friendly technician. My inability to say much or smile tells her that I'm uncomfortable. She tries chatting me up about the weather and the upcoming university football game. Smiling, I think, *Who cares?*

Bill and I take the elevator up to the clinic. We enter a huge room that feels like a sports arena. It's filled with people waiting to see their oncologists. Again, the PA is loudly calling the names of those who are next in line to see their doctors. Young women, who strike me as volunteers, whisk them away to offices down long, dark hallways.

I can't keep my tears at bay. Those of us waiting have deer-in-headlights eyes. We're about to find out whether we're going to live or die. No one is smiling or happy. We just sit and follow whom we're told to follow and don't ask questions. I am trapped and will never get out. Bill is talking to me, trying to keep me from running. I feel as though I'm waiting for the guillotine to take my head off. But what is it I'm guilty of? If I have to sit here much longer, I'm going to vomit all over the place.

Finally, we're in Dr. C.'s small office space. She looks to be in her early thirties and has a fantastic reputation for her surgical work. I wonder how someone so young can know so much. Her smile is contagious, her voice is soothing, and I calm down a bit. I try to tell her how I'm feeling, but I'm not sure she gets how threatening this place is to me. She examines me, and we set a date for surgery. She reassures me that the type of cancer I have is easy to remove and the odds of its ever returning are minuscule.

After surgery, three weeks later, I wake up in a dark room. The door is ajar, and I notice soft light somewhere in the distance. I'm connected to a machine delivering fluids to my body. Another is supplying me with oxygen. Something wrapped around my legs keeps inflating and deflating. When I ask the nurse what it's for, she tells me it keeps blood clots from forming. Oh, yes—Mom had one of those on her leg as she was dying.

I'm terribly thirsty and in pain, and my brain is thick with fog. The leftover anesthesia in my body is making me feel worse than the pain from the surgery. I keep drifting in and out of consciousness, and the nurse keeps waking me every hour to take my vital signs and make sure I'm doing okay. I ask her to go away and leave me alone, but she tells me she can't.

Later, as daylight enters through the small window behind my bed, I'm more awake and aware. I'm in a closet-size room in an older section of the hospital. It's painted a dark, dingy gray. I tell the nurse I want to go home, but she says I can't. I need to stay until all of my bodily functions are working properly, meaning I need to be able to pee and poop without any problems.

I'm not terribly happy. But when several nurses come just to talk to me, I start smiling. They are full of life and eager to make me feel better. One sings to me, another tells jokes, and another tells me about her life and how grateful to God she is for helping her through difficult times. I'm taken by their warmth and caring. Before long, I'm laughing along with them. I wish I could take these angelic beings home with me. I love their spirit, their kindness, the love they have for their patients and for all of life.

Later in the day, once I'm at home in my own bed, Dr. C. calls to tell me that not only was she able to successfully remove all of my reproductive organs, but all of the cancer is gone as well. I'm delighted and have no problem with having lost those things. I'm too old to be using fallopian tubes and the rest of that stuff. Now that I've said good riddance to the cancer, I have a whole new shot at making my life the best it can be.

# VISITING *the* PAST

*December 2010*

I'M TAKING SHORT WALKS AROUND HOME, AND I RETURN to Pilates class. Even though we're fairly new in the neighborhood, the people I meet on my walks tell me how happy they are that I'm doing well and continue to ask if there is anything they can do for me. Even the idea that Christmas is upon us doesn't shake my mood or my gratitude for just being alive. Given this chance to come back from the land of depression and angst, I know I can handle most anything. If I ever had doubts about Bill's love for me, they are gone. His care has been phenomenal. I will always carry my appreciation of him and all of those who have supported me.

As the days pass, the need to share the enormous changes going on in my life is growing. The idea of writing a memoir is still kicking around in my head, but it's still just a tiny seed that needs a bit more fertilizer and water. I've removed my cloak of victimhood, ripped it to shreds, and extinguished the need to blame others for my problems. I'm a survivor. Nothing can take me down. Not my mother. Not cancer. I'm the only one with the power to destroy me. And that is something I have no intention of doing.

Astonishing epiphanies arrive in loud *aha!* moments; others arrive quietly, on tiptoe, in my dreams. One dream in particular, about visiting my childhood homes on Long Island, sparks action. When I wake up, I'm happy and smiling. I never thought that returning to those places, where I often found life more than difficult, was something I'd want to do. But now I think it may be something I *need* to do. I want to let the sun shine on the bits and pieces of myself that I left behind in those dark corners of my past life. But it also frightens me. Do I have the guts to actually go back and take a look around to see where I came from? Is there anything that remains in those places that I need to revisit? If there is, what shall I say to it?

TWO MONTHS LATER, BILL AND I fly to New York and see a few shows in the city. We rent a car and drive out onto the island. This isn't a trip I want to do on my own. I'm worried that if I went by myself I'd get scared and quit before I'm done. Bill is beside me in case I need a hand to hold, should the journey get gnarly. He will be a witness for me. I'll be able to speak out loud and share things that come back to me. If I start building barriers that block my path, his presence will help to keep me moving forward.

Driving around my old territory, I'm excited but also a bit frustrated because I can't seem to locate all of the homes I lived in. Things have changed dramatically since I lived here. Gone are the potato fields that the island was once covered with. They're replaced by unending subdivisions and strip malls. At first I don't recognize the house in Commack, where I lived when I was in fourth and fifth grade. I remember it being so much bigger than it really is. Now it looks tiny and is enclosed in a tangle of trees and vines that have taken over the open space it once occupied. The Carvel that was located on Jericho Turnpike, just across from the entrance to my street, is gone. So is the drive-in theater behind it, where I cried through the movie *Shane*.

Out on Eaton's Neck, where I lived during my high school years, the population has boomed, but in the building of new homes, the oak and maple trees have been left untouched and the landscape is still as lush as ever. The house my father built for us is still there, newly expanded and painted. I can still hear the voices of my friends echoing through the years, as we swam in the sluice and gathered apples and blackberries that we made into pies and sold to raise enough money so that we could go to Coney Island together for an end-of-summer blast before school started again.

Despite all the physical and emotional violence that happened to me here, this is the place I loved most. It was here that I first got a glimpse of who I could become if given a chance. When my father decided to sell his business and our house and move us to Vermont in 1960, after I graduated from high school, I was bereft. I didn't want to leave the place I was finally able to call home. I would miss my circle of trusted friends. A year later, after my freshman year in college, I returned to Long Island to work, looking for the old magic. Unfortunately, it was gone. My closest friends had gone off to college or moved away.

Bill and I have made a reservation to spend the night at an inn that used to be the home of my friend Nick. He lived in the city during the school year. This was his summer home, an old Victorian mansion just a two-minute walk from my house. It must have been one of the first houses built out on this spit of land surrounded by water. We were never boyfriend and girlfriend, just good friends. I was actually head over heels for Richard, the drummer in Nick's band, which practiced in the foyer of his house several evenings a week.

As we drive up to check in, it looks exactly as I remember it. I begin to get shaky. A bit teary, I tell Bill, "I don't think I want to spend the night here after all."

Bill asks, "Why? I think we should go inside and see how it feels. Who knows how you might feel once you walk through the door?"

I counter, "I can't. I'm afraid of ghosts. I've already stepped over a line that was drawn in the sand when I moved away. This whole thing is scary. I want to take my time before I walk any further into the past."

In Port Jefferson, where I was born and had my tonsils removed, the hospital has expanded. Except for the small dome on the original building, I would never know it as the same place. The two-room school I went to is gone, as is my grandparents' small farm, where I learned how to pluck chickens and make the best chicken soup in the world. The potato fields that surrounded it have been taken over by high-end, cookie-cutter homes. I was very young when I lived here, and every turn in the road renders me completely lost.

In Huntington we find the alpine-style home my father

built. The small, Tudor-style building that was once the library, where I learned about the joy of reading, is also still there. I remember how safe and comfortable I felt there, in the peace and quiet. I'd sit in one of the window seats, perusing books while tiny flecks of dust swam through the rays of sun surrounding me. It now houses the offices of the Veterans of Foreign Wars.

Bill again suggests I go into the building to see what they've done to it. But I have an aversion to going inside any of these places. I don't mind peeking in windows, but actually entering makes my stomach squirm.

We drive by the hospital where I gave up my appendix, and the church where I received my First Holy Communion. That church is where my parents were told they were living in sin. The pain of rejection I felt there is still palpable.

IT ISN'T UNTIL DAYS LATER, when I'm back in Virginia, that I realize just how important this trip was for me. Because I'm not one to attend class reunions or events of that kind, going back and risking feeling the awful pain of those years was a courageous act. It took a boldness I didn't know I had to connect with a part of me that I had tried to forget about. Had I not gone, I would not have discovered that I am not a broken, defective person. The memories I've been hiding from myself contained some of the happiest moments of my life, despite the abuse and trauma that went along with them. I'm able to see it all in a different light now. Though my parents had their own issues, I believe they tried to do the best they could. They did love me. It's just that life can be cruel. Mom and Dad had their own traumas to sort through and didn't have the tools that are available to me today. They simply didn't know any better.

I've recovered the little girl who still grasps my hand too tightly when she is afraid. When we left Long Island together, so many years ago, she was just beginning to grow up. Since then, I have ignored her. She stopped growing as I got taller and moved on. I locked her away because she was too needy. Now it's time for me to give her the attention she deserves. I'll start by paying attention to how she feels, allowing her to be afraid or happy, and making sure she always feels safe.

# 35

## THE FINAL BURIAL

*October 2012*

GOING THROUGH SECURITY, I RAISE MY HANDS OVER my head. I can't see the X-ray image of my body that shows up on the screen, but it confirms that I'm not carrying a bomb, a knife, a gun, or any other threatening weapon. A smiling TSA agent waves me on. But another agent, noticing a dark, rectangular object on the X-ray that scans luggage on the conveyer belt, stops my carry-on for a second look. She hands it to yet another agent, who asks me to follow her over to a table. They want to know what that is tucked inside my bag. She says it's too dense to see through and asks permission to open it—as if I have a choice.

I watch, giggling to myself, as she unzips the bag and slowly wipes around the edges with a swab that can detect particles of dangerous substances. The test shows I haven't been playing with anything harmful to my fellow passengers or myself. Then, lifting a sweater off the top layer inside the bag, she spots the brown plastic box. She lifts it out slowly and carefully, as if it might bite her. My grin widens as I tell her what's inside. "It's my mom," I say, as she carefully opens the box to reveal a plastic bag filled with gray ashes. She smiles apologetically, telling me she has to scan the bag, the box, and the ashes once again —"just to double-check."

I wait by the table as she stops others going through security, placing my bag and Mom on the belt so that they can be rescanned. I hear Mom laughing as the agent hands her back to me, apologizing for the inconvenience. I thank her for making sure we'll be flying safely, repack Mom carefully, and head to the gate for my flight to New York.

The next morning, Bill and I wake to clouds and rain. We are back on Long Island to scatter what's left of Mom's ashes, after she's spent five years cooped up in a variety of closets, never seeing the light of day. Just before we left home, we scattered a handful of her in the garden so that we could keep her near. The rest I'll scatter in the places she loved, on the south and north shores of Long Island, where she was born in 1923 and lived until our family moved to Vermont in 1960.

We'll begin in Oakdale, where she and Dad bought a house after the move to New England. Mom hated the long, dark winters that Vermont is so well known for. She wanted a place to escape to warmer climes, where she could be close to extended family and old friends.

I have visited that particular house only once or twice and can't remember the exact address. It's been at least forty years since I last set foot here. Many things have changed, including the landscape. There are buildings where before there were woods, and many more houses. I'll have to depend on intuitive memory hits and visual clues.

I know the house is on the banks of the Connetquot River, which feeds into Great South Bay. On a Google map, we locate Shore Drive. It's the only street that runs along the river. We slowly make our way through quiet, tree-lined streets, eventually turning onto the road where Mom once lived. At a mailbox marked 148, my memory flashes red. The lights grow brighter, and as we get closer, I'm sure it's right there in front of me. But because I don't recognize the house, now hidden behind dense trees and shrubbery, we slowly drive the length of the street to see if there are other possibilities. We turn around after I receive no other hits.

It's raining, cold, and blustery. Bill slowly drives back to the house that first caught my attention. There are a few people on the street, going about their business. I'm worried someone will call the cops if they see a strange car in the neighborhood spreading a powdery substance along the street. When no one appears to be looking, I carefully open my window, dangle my arm innocently out the window, and sift handfuls of ashes through my fingers along the way. But because the window is down, the wind blows ashes back in my face and the inside of the car starts getting dusty. The fire-engine-red of my rain jacket begins to turn a strange shade of pink. Bill and I howl with laughter.

We stop again at number 148, where I let go of another few handfuls. I leave more up the street, along a canal where several boats are moored. I feel compelled to scatter Mom everywhere. She deeply loved this place. I envision her perched on the hood of our car, smiling and waving like the queen she was, as bits and pieces of her settle onto the ground.

As I roll up the window, I realize we're supposed to meet my cousin at her home in twenty minutes. I haven't seen her since Bill and I were married in Vermont, forty-seven years ago. I'm covered with my mother's remains, as are the seat and floor of the car around me. I panic. Joanne will surely think I'm loony if she sees me like this. We stop for baby wipes to clean up the ashes before I walk back into her life.

Joanne greets us at her front door. We share a long, tight hug. She guides us on a visit to a nearby cemetery, where our grandparents, on our mothers' side, are buried. It's a Catholic cemetery, and I'm told that the scattering of ashes is forbidden here. It's okay if you bury them, but scattering, for some reason, is not allowed. The recovering Catholic who I am has different ideas.

In the process of reclaiming and reintegrating every piece of my being that has been split apart through the years, I'm about to break another holy Roman Catholic law. I wish to recognize and make peace with my ancestors, and with whom and what they brought forth into the world. Mom and I are both results of their union. They are our people. Placing a small handful of Mom's ashes here will bring us all together, providing healing for long-forgotten abuses over the years. Mom's parents caused much rage and many ugly disputes throughout their lives, but I want to honor them for the life they gifted to me. And so, in the cold drizzle, I scatter several handfuls of Mom on the green grass where my grandma and grandpa sleep.

After lunch, Bill and I head to Patchogue, where Mom lived for years before she married my dad. Her address was 15 South Street. We locate numbers 12 and 14. They are ancient, crumbling homes soon to be razed for a complex of medical offices.

Number 15 was obviously across the street, but now there is only a large vacant lot filled with weeds and beer cans. I scatter more ashes there, before we drive around the corner to the high school Mom attended for only one year. I sprinkle a handful of ashes among the shrubs in front of the old brick building.

Tired and chilled to the bone, Bill and I head back to our hotel. We'll finish scattering Mom's remaining ashes tomorrow. I'm already beginning to feel lighter, and I look forward to completing this ritual I've put together. I'm not one for rites and ceremonies, but I'm discovering there are necessary exceptions. Most seem empty to me, too solemn, too formal. This observance of letting go is anything but solemn. I find myself laughing much of the time, with brief bouts of tears mixed in for good measure. I'm feeling deep love for my mother, who during her last years was anything but lovable. I'd love for my family to remember me in this way when I die.

The following day is sunny and much warmer. We drive to the north shore, to a beach where Mom often took my brothers and me clamming. At low tide, one huge sandbar dominated a small cove just off the Sound. We'd walk, scanning the wet sand for tiny holes that gave away the presence of clams waiting to fill our dinner plates. On hands and knees we'd dig deep, tossing our finds, mostly longneck clams, into our buckets.

At home, Mom steamed them and served them in a large bowl in the center of the kitchen table. We'd fill our plates, then dip the meat from the now-opened shells in melted butter spiked with lots of garlic. This meal, along with freshly picked corn on the cob and huge helpings of a tossed summer salad, was always the high point of the week.

Today the tide is high, so there will be no searching for

clams or for an old, battered pair of eyeglasses that my brother Zed lost here many years ago. I toss ashes along the shoreline before crossing the road to the pavilion, standing in a large grove of oak trees. I hear a square dance caller singing out instructions to promenade or do-si-do. I see Mom and Dad sashaying about the floor with their friends, to the sound of old-time hoedown music blaring from a black Victrola.

My brothers and I are playing with other kids, chasing lightning bugs and playing tag in the dark. We feast on sweet watermelon, spitting the small, dark seeds from our mouths, each of us hoping to become the long-distance seed-spitting champion of the night. I dust the ground with more ashes here, where we spent many memorable summer evenings so long ago.

Later, we search for Holy Cross Polish National Cemetery in Commack, where my dad's father is buried. Tucked under a stand of maple and oak trees, the cemetery is dark and foreboding, like my memories of my grandfather. It is a lonely burial ground where only Polish Catholics are buried. There is no caretaker about. All of the spaces have long been filled. I leave a small white stone on the top of Dziadzia's gravestone to mark my visit. Babcia, his wife, is buried in California, so there is no including her on this trip.

Dziadzia, a large, balding, dark-complected man, had very few grandfatherly skills. I was terribly afraid of him, and of my grandmother Babcia. They spoke often of the big, bad wolf that lived in the springhouse across the street from their house. He'd eat children, they warned, if they didn't eat the food placed in front of them at mealtime.

Since Dziadzia is an ancestor who provided me with life, I feel compelled to include him in my peacemaking journey.

However, I don't leave Mom's ashes here. She'd be back to haunt me for sure if I did. There was nothing more than a painful tolerance between them, and hints from several cousins have led me to believe that he may have tried to sexually abuse young girls and unsuspecting women.

In Northport, where I graduated from high school, we stop for ice cream at the soda fountain where I spent much of my time after school. It's still run by members of the same family that started the business in 1929. I sit on a stool at the black marble counter, which I doubt has been replaced since I lived here. To honor Mom, I order homemade lemon-custard ice cream drizzled with hot fudge sauce, one of her favorite treats.

Our final destination, and for me the most evocative location on this journey, is Eaton's Neck. Though I recently visited here, my head is overflowing with a new mix of memories: being beaten by my father; learning to tell lies; my first serious boyfriend, whose kisses melted my heart; and the warm, gentle summers I spent swimming, waterskiing, and finding my way through puberty. It was a place of great suffering for me, a small, battered child who survived the clashing tides, as well as constant threats of extinction. Yet within the pain and fear I experienced, there were moments of quiet sweetness, joy, and great learning.

We pause to scatter ashes at the home where I lived. Built by my father, it was one of his finest creations. Its three stories are tucked into the side of a hill, just above a tidal inlet. At low tide the air is filled with a pungent, organic smell, both fetid and pleasing, imparting the cycle of life and the knowing that one is close to the origin of all things. In the tidal mud, fecund cells constantly divide and multiply, and the miracle of birth gives way to constant change and the finality of death.

I could never think of living here again. Its early magic is gone, like my youth. But part of my heart still resides here.

For the final rite of letting go, we stop at a small private beach on the Sound that my family once owned. The sky is a deep, arctic blue. A few feathery clouds drift from the west. I empty the last of Mom's gritty ashes into gentle swells as they touch the shore. She is absorbed back into the salty sea from whence we all came. I wish her well, tell her I miss her, and blow a kiss into the air. It's a perfect day, a perfect place, and I completely accept her into my heart.

A FEW MONTHS LATER, AS I was doing a major cleanup of my studio, I discovered a small tin sitting on a windowsill I rarely dust. When I opened it, I found more ashes, along with a small piece of paper tucked on top that read, "Mom." I laughed and sprinkled them outside my studio door in a bed of hellebores and peonies. Once again, as she often did, Mom had the last word. But this time, instead of feeling annoyed by her, I welcomed her words and said, "Thank you."

I do miss her. She was a good person, trying to do the best that she could. She often made mistakes and fell down. But she always got back up again and moved forward.

If anyone had told me in 2007, when Mom died, that I would transform my life from one of victimhood, hatred, and anger into one of joy, peace, and acceptance, I would have told them, "Never." I was firmly planted in a pit of quicksand, slowly drowning in a life of guilt and shame, up to my eyeballs in hatred for the woman who brought me into the world.

Letting go of the past has taught me that broken ties are creations of the mind, to which we add continuous levels of story. We rework them as we move through life, remembering only the darkest of times. By releasing my mother from the prison I built for her, I've liberated myself from a life of closed doors. Living with anger, resentment, and hatred, I had constructed a cell not only for her but for myself. By revisiting the past and my relationship with Mom, I've shined bright light into the darkest corners, where I had hidden my pain. Not only have I found forgiveness for her, I've found it for myself.

# EPILOGUE

*December 2014*

HERE I AM AT THE END OF THIS WRITING. DURING the process, memories have come to the surface, and the puzzle pieces of my life, as they connect with my mother, have come together. Looking back and remembering what I tried so hard to forget has gone a long way in healing the brokenness I have felt for so long. To be able to see my feelings appear on the screen in front of me, and then to watch them change over time as I rewrite, edit, and heal, is magical. It's like being able to watch the day-by-day knitting together of a broken bone.

I have come a long way in accepting myself. My journey continues when I wake up every morning, put my feet on the ground, and start moving. I will always make mistakes, but I'll try my best to fix them. I will most likely still have fits of temper and meltdowns, and react if a juicy trigger comes my way. But when it does, I now know what's happening. I'm quick to catch myself and count to ten or twenty. I can then back down before my reaction creates pandemonium. I'm choosing my battles much more carefully these days and find it exhilarating to be able to say "No!" to the dragon who still resides inside me and who wants to heat up the world when she feels threatened.

As I watched my mother struggle as she died, I knew I

wanted ease not only in my life but in death as well. I want my departure to be a clean sweep. I want the time I've spent here on Earth to be about the spirit of kindness and about taking my lessons seriously. Going to places on my bucket list, like Mongolia or Australia, is not as important to me as leaving the world a better place than it was when I arrived.

For years I have struggled with the concept of forgiveness. If I forgave my parents for their abuse, I believed I'd forget the harsh sting of my father's horse crop on my legs and the prayers I screamed inside my head, begging Mom to come to my rescue. I kept it all a secret for a long time, afraid of the hurt yet haunted by my muteness.

But forgiveness is not about forgetting. It's about understanding those who have done us harm and their inability, for whatever reason, to stop their own behavior. I will never forget how my parents treated me, but knowing that my mother was severely abused as a child and that my father suffered from PTSD is the key to my forgiving them.

I've also had to forgive myself. I've chosen not to forget the times I have been mean, cruel, and hurtful to those around me. Those rememberings keep me honest. I can never set an example of how to live a clean life if my own windows are dirty and garbage is piling up outside my door. I am human. I make mistakes. I will always need to make amends to those I hurt and to be kind to myself, even when I do something unkind.

All of this learning has taken time. It comes and goes in waves. Just when I breathe a sigh of relief, thinking I've learned a lesson, the problem often reappears in another form. When there is anger involved, I know I haven't done my homework properly.

It's easy to learn not to touch a hot stove when we feel the excruciating pain and see the blisters forming. But learning that anger won't help us to solve our problems is much more difficult. Anger can make us feel good for a while. Expressing it out loud feels like getting revenge and can get a load off our shoulders, but only for a moment. It always comes back to haunt us, often in the form of shame.

Inviting Mom to live with me helped me to grow into the person I am today: strong, happy, and able to take care of any difficulty that might arise. I never would have been able to start making changes and to take responsibility for myself without our time together. I never would have learned that my mother was simply another human being, just like me. Without her, I'd never have known that hatred can turn into love.

Now, eight years after her death, life continues to bring new lessons. I've gotten older as these words were written. I further understand who Mom became as she aged, and the often difficult stages our bodies go through as our systems wind down.

Don't get me wrong, I'm cancer-free and healthy as can be, but I notice how much more forgetful I am than I was just a few years ago. Getting down on the floor to play with my dogs and then standing up tall and straight is much harder than it used to be. I'm learning how to take better care of myself so that I can be comfortable as the years pass and I step into the shoes of those who went before me.

In October 2014, I made another trip to Vermont, to visit family and to inspect the stone that I had ordered and placed next to my father's in the cemetery in Hanover, New Hampshire. It has Mom's name on it and her birth and death dates. It sits in an open area of the cemetery where the sun reaches it all day long during fair weather. On that day, two white-tailed does were grazing nearby, the leaves were at their peak of fall color, and I finally found the peace and closure I've been yearning for since my mother died. The long road to recovery has been filled with pain and terrifying pinnacles I never thought I'd be able to conquer, but living with adversity does have its gifts.

# ACKNOWLEDGMENTS

Writing a book isn't a solo proposition. Many folks along the way helped to encourage me and get this job done. There was Sharon Martinelli, who saw my stories as a book long before I started writing it. My writing coach, Kevin Quirk, met with me every other week, read the trash I sent him, asked questions, made me find answers, and kept me going when I wanted to quit. My beta readers, Jane Barnes, Sue Hoar, Kathy Pooler, and Shirley Showalter, supported me all the way and continue to cheer me on.

And to Brooke Warner and all of the folks at She Writes Press, I send Kudos for the work you do in helping women like me to bring their stories out into the world. I will always be grateful to Annie Tucker, my editor, who saw the potential in my work and never tried to make my story into something it wasn't. Caitlin Hamilton Summie made the road to marketing smoother than I ever felt possible. I love you all.

Of course, there would be no book without the love, support, and encouragement I got from Bill, the love of my life, and my little dogs, Sam and Max, who slept at my feet during much of the writing. To them, and to the innumerable others who have shown interest in this project, I send unending thanks, love, and hope that you will enjoy what you have helped me to create.

## ABOUT *the* AUTHOR

photo credit: Martyn Kayle

JOAN Z. ROUGH is a visual artist, poet, and writer of nonfiction. Her photographs and paintings have been exhibited around the United States. Her poetry has been published in a variety of journals and is included in the anthology *Some Say Tomato*, by Mariflo Stephens. Joan's first book, *Australian Locker Hooking: A New Approach to a Traditional Craft*, was published in 1982. When she's not working in her studio, you can find her in her garden, trimming roses. She lives in Charlottesville, Virginia, with her husband, Bill, and their rescued dogs, Sam and Max.

## SELECTED TITLES FROM SHE WRITES PRESS

She Writes Press is an independent publishing company founded to serve women writers everywhere. Visit us at www.shewritespress.com.

*Don't Call Me Mother: A Daughter's Journey from Abandonment to Forgiveness* by Linda Joy Myers. $16.95, 978-1-938314-02 -5. Linda Joy Myers's story of how she transcended the prisons of her childhood by seeking—and offering—forgiveness for her family's sins.

*Don't Leave Yet: How My Mother's Alzheimer's Opened My Heart* by Constance Hanstedt. $16.95, 978-1-63152-952-8. The chronicle of Hanstedt's journey toward independence, self-assurance, and connectedness as she cares for her mother, who is rapidly losing her own identity to the early stage of Alzheimer's.

*The Space Between: A Memoir of Mother-Daughter Love at the End of Life* by Virginia A. Simpson. $16.95, 978-1-63152-049-5. When a life-threatening illness makes it necessary for Virginia Simpson's mother, Ruth, to come live with her, Simpson struggles to heal their relationship before Ruth dies.

*All the Ghosts Dance Free: A Memoir* by Terry Cameron Baldwin. $16.95, 978-1-63152-822-4. A poetic memoir that explores the legacy of alcoholism and teen suicide in one woman's life—and her efforts to create an authentic existence in the face of that legacy.

*Fourteen: A Daughter's Memoir of Adventure, Sailing, and Survival* by Leslie Johansen Nack. $16.95, 978-1-63152-941-2. A coming-of-age adventure story about a young girl who comes into her own power, fights back against abuse, becomes an accomplished sailor, and falls in love with the ocean and the natural world.

*Secrets in Big Sky Country: A Memoir* by Mandy Smith. $16.95, 978-1-63152-814-9. A bold and unvarnished memoir about the shattering consequences of familial sexual abuse—and the strength it takes to overcome them.